The World Book of Greatness 2020

Greatness University

Greatness University Publishers
info@greatness-university.com
www.greatness-university.com

ISBN: 978-1-913164-71-3
ISBN-13: 978-1-913164-71-3

GREATNESS UNIVERSITY

LONDON, UK

Contents

Welcome to the World Book of Greatness

"Sometimes it falls upon a generation to be great, you can be that generation." Nelson Mandela

Thank you for choosing to read the World Book of Greatness: the world's first and only official record of great people. This book is curated by Greatness University: world's first institution dedicated to discovering, developing and delivering greatness in individuals and organisations.

As dedicated greatness creators, our team members, business partners and global ambassadors are always researching, rewarding and celebrating greatness. Our goal is to help people step into their greatness faster than they can ever imagine through our breakthrough education, revolutionary training methods, and prestigious unconventional awards. Thank you for taking time to read about these great people. We hope their stories will inspire you to walk into your greatness so that you increase your influence and affluence. This is your season to be an example and not an exception of greatness. This is your time to join the greatness generation. As founder, I Professor Patrick Businge take this opportunity to welcome you to our Greatness Planet. Allow me now to introduce to you Greatness University.

Breakthrough Education

Greatness University offers the breakthrough education the world has been waiting for: an education that helps people discover, develop and deliver their greatness. Greatness university has been very fortunate to work on this cutting-edge education model for the past 3 years. This breakthrough education which synchronies real-time greatness, impactful authorship, and traditional academia is delivered through its virtual institutes and affiliate partners globally.

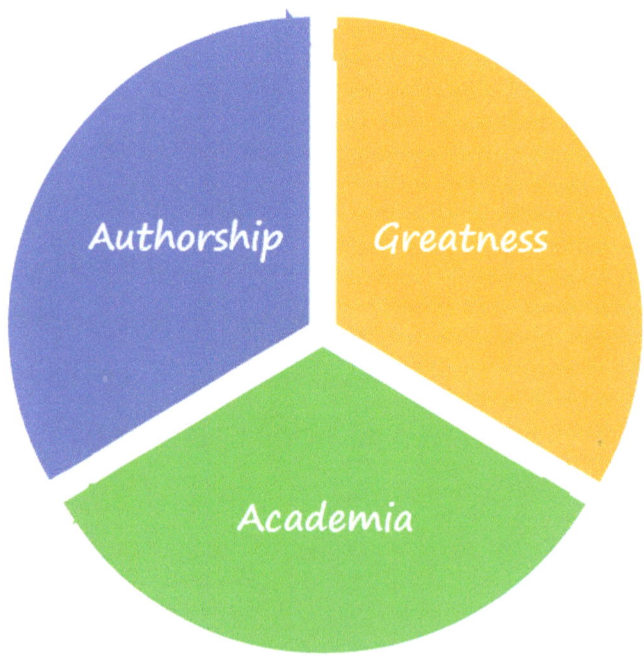

Greatnisation Institute	We believe there are great people in our generation. This belief is the fountain of our unparalleled work at the Greatnisation Institute where we do anthological and biographical research on greatness. This is where the World Book of Greatness is curated and the World Greatness Awards are managed.
Greatness Research Institute	We know your greatness could be stalled or destroyed by being in the wrong environment. Greatness Research Institute provides you a space where you can discover, develop, deliver and sustain your greatness through coaching, mentoring, research and training.
Royal Studies Institute	You are royalty. There is nothing painful than having royalty buried inside you. Your royalty is too valuable to go unnoticed when you are gone. Through our discover your royalty coaching, modern day royalty training and royal fashion and design, we will help you unleash your royalty and brand you as a modern day royal.

Authorship Studies Institute	Welcome to the Authorship Studies Institute: the space where great authors are born. Here you will engage in the creative process of writing so that you publish your book. Emphasis will be placed on process as much as product. The notion of 'work in progress' will be a major focus with frequent opportunities for you to present your work in workshops or discuss it on a one-to-one basis with your book writing mentor in order to gain feedback. Our innovative courses are enhanced by research, online activities and masterclasses by acclaimed authors, editors and publishers from a range of genres. These will support you plan, write, publish, and market your book; and explore the possibility of you becoming an authorpreneur.
Rewrite Your Future Institute	The great Dr Myles Monroe once said, "Discontent is the seed of change. You will never change what you tolerate." Rewrite Your Future Institute is dedicated to consultancy for individuals, kingdoms, businesses, governmental and non-governmental organisations so that they change what they tolerate. Here you will get the confidence to repair your life, reright your present, rewrite your future, and recreate your greatness so that you walk into every season of life prepared.

Greatness Publications

Can you imagine your book being launched at a Coronation Ceremony in one of our partner kingdoms, being exhibited at a World Book Fair or being given as a gift to a head of state? At Greatness University, we will help you publish your work with Greatness University Publications. This publishing arm includes: *Greatness University Publishers* for books, the *Royalty Press* for news, *Greatness University Journals* for articles, and the *World Book of Greatness* for profiles and biographies. Through Greatness University Publications, you will get the global exposure and influence you deserve. For a list of our publications, visit www.greatness-university.com

World Greatness Day

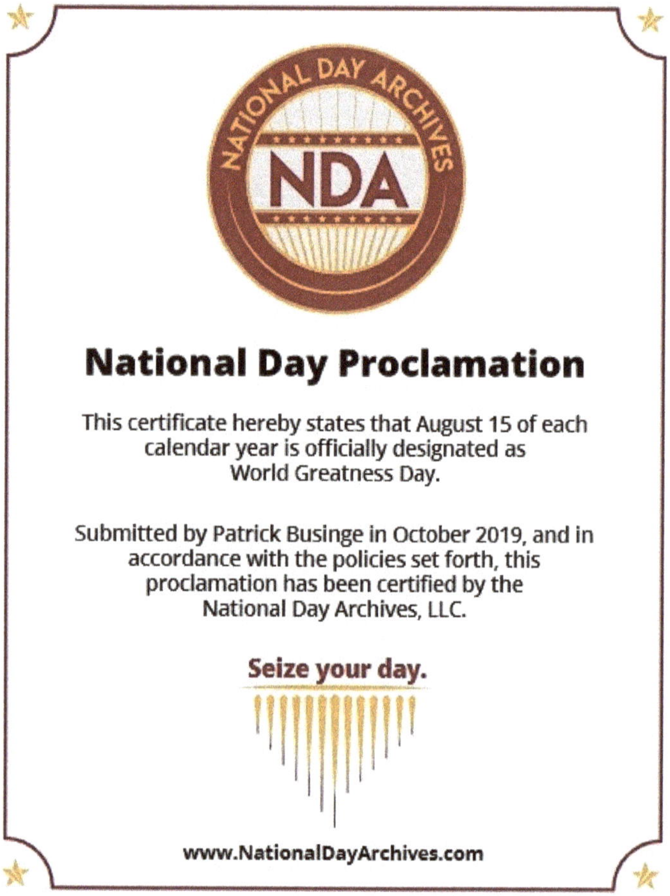

National Day Proclamation

This certificate hereby states that August 15 of each calendar year is officially designated as World Greatness Day.

Submitted by Patrick Businge in October 2019, and in accordance with the policies set forth, this proclamation has been certified by the National Day Archives, LLC.

Seize your day.

www.NationalDayArchives.com

The world is filled with unsung heroes and heroines. More often, their greatness is never celebrated when they are alive. Very often, their greatness is talked about when they are dead especially in their eulogies.

The *World Greatness Day* is an occasion to recognise, honour and celebrate people who have helped us to positively change our lives whilst they are alive. It is celebrated in all countries around the world through festivals, gatherings, parties, award ceremonies, talks, lectures, visits, and many other ways to express gratitude to great people in our lives. For more information, visit https://www.nationaldayarchives.com/day/world-greatness-day/ or get in touch to explore how you too can host the World Greatness Day in your country.

World Book of Greatness

This is the only and first ever book that documents great people. When you receive your award from Greatness University, your name and biography are inscribed in the World Book of Greatness. This is the place to go and find out what is happening in the Greatness Planet. Email us at info@greatness-university.com and we will send you a digital copy when it comes out.

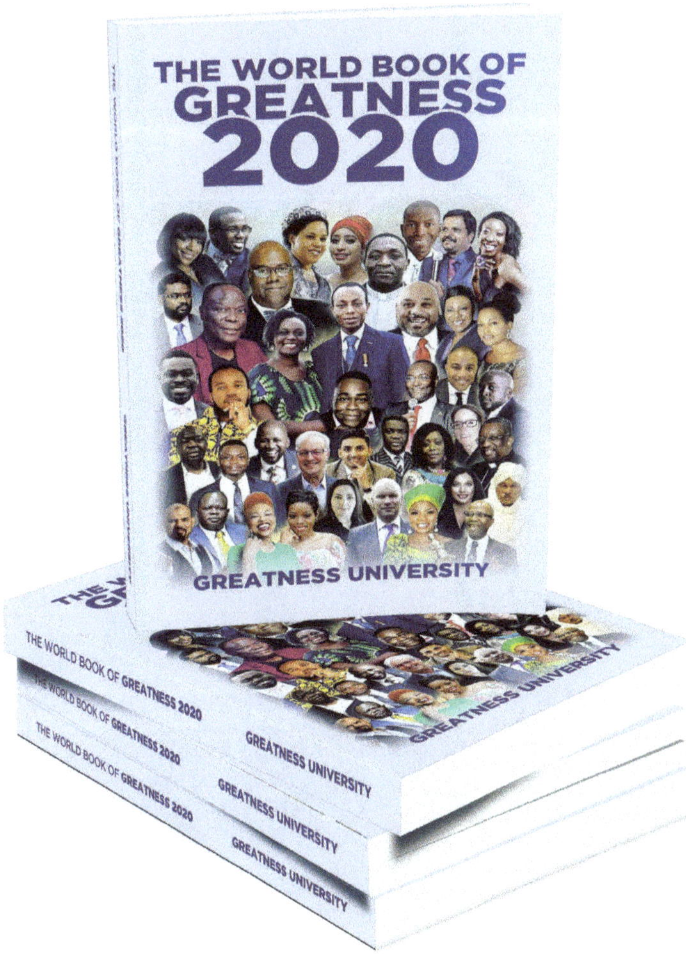

World Greatness Awards

"Your life is an example and not an exception of greatness"

In a planet where most people live in the sea of sameness, we look out for people who are doing ordinary things in extraordinary ways. To appreciate their tireless service for being leading lights, creators, authors, legends, researchers, masters, and icons of greatness, we recognise their unparalleled contribution to practice, academia and to the publishing world with a variety of our prestigious honorary, unconventional and legacy awards.

Our prestigious greatness awards are already changing the way we appreciate the greatness that is in our midst. Our unconventional awards are given on merit upon approval by the awards board based on the criteria below.

Categories	Criteria
Seeker of Greatness	You know your identity and you are on the journey of self-mastery
Finder of Greatness	You have identified your mission in life and you are courageously living your purpose
Visionary of Greatness	You have a great vision for the world and you are attracting followers in your community
Teacher of Greatness	You have guided your students from the darkness of ignorance into the light of knowledge
Master of Greatness	You have mastered your greatness and are helping others to do the same
Researcher of Greatness	You have researched greatness with Greatness University Research Institute
Author of Greatness	You have written and published a book with Greatness University Publishers

Creator of Greatness	You are consistently engaged in positive action and you are transforming your community
Doctor of Greatness	You are a change maker, entrepreneur, influencer, and practitioner who has mastered your craft.
Icon of Greatness	You have served humanity and you are a living example of selfless service
Leading Light of Greatness	You are a leading light that is shining brightly and attracting followers from various parts of the world.
Voice of Greatness	You are an activist who has given his life to speak for others so that you transform their reality
Professor of Greatness	You are an influencer, practitioner, academic who has gone where there is no path and created a trail.
The Professor Patrick Businge Greatness Award	You have personally been mentored by our founder or you emulate his example by your life and actions
Legend of Greatness	You have replicated greatness and your legacy has been documented by Greatness University

The World Greatness Awards 2020

London Luton Hoo 25th January 2020

Sponsors & Hosts for World Greatness Awards

Peace Apartments is your home away from home. We provide affordable, modern, quality, comfortable and self-catering accommodation in Luton: 30 minutes away from central London. During your stay you, will have your own kitchenette, get free Wi-Fi, and have access to a fully equipped gym.

Dr Raymond Harlall

Connect at www.raymondharlall.com and get published in his series

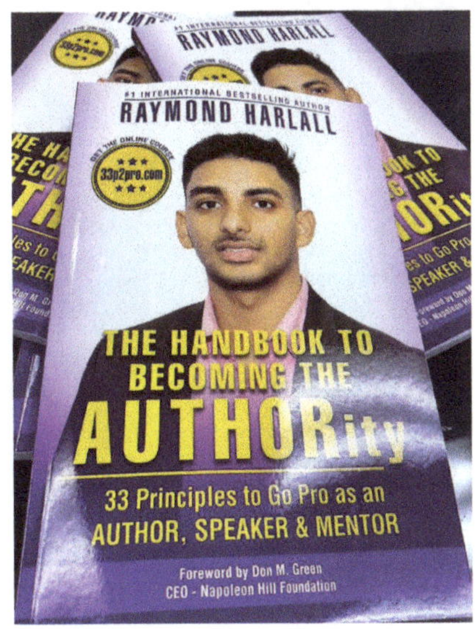

The Fahy Brothers, UK

Thanks to the Fahy Brothers: Damian and Peter for providing the entertainment on the first World Greatness Awards tonight. The Fahy Brothers have been on big stages like Buckingham Palace in London where they played for Queen Elizabeth II and have recorded their music at the Legendary Sun Studios in Memphis Tennessee: the birthplace of Rock 'N' Roll where legends like Johnny Cash, Elvis Presley, Jerry Lee Lewis and Howling Wolf did their recording.

The Fahy Brothers at performing at Buckingham Palace, London

The Fahy Brothers recording at Sun Studios in Memphis Tennessee

Dr Julian Businge, UK

Founder of Peace Property Education, Award-winning Speaker, Author, and Co-Founder of World Greatness Awards

www.julianbusinge.com

Julian Businge is a successful entrepreneur. She is the Founder and CEO of Peace Property Education: a firm that specialises in serviced accommodation commonly known as Airbnb. Through this firm, she offers mentoring and coaching services to women looking for time and financial freedom. Together with her husband, co-founded Peace Apartments in 2016, which operates short term accommodation the London suburb of Luton, UK.

Julian Businge is a Royal Fashions Expert who is creative, caring and customer focused. Her project in 2019 has been working closely with the Queen Mother of Tooro in Uganda to create Royal fashions and design. This is aimed at blending tradition and modernity and create modern-day cultural wear.

Julian Businge is a published author. She has authored and co-authored many books about property and business including:

- *Increase Your Cash Flow: Serviced Accommodation* where she teaches how to make money through property
- *Breakthrough Declarations of a Praying Wife* where she teaches how to pray for our family members
- *Yega Orutooro: Learn Rutooro Language* which is a resource to help children living in diaspora learn their local language.

Julian Businge has been privileged to be coached and mentored by legends like Les Brown, the World's Number 1 Motivational Speaker and His Excellency Dr. Clyde Rivers, Ambassador at Large for Burundi and Founder of IChange Nations. With their help and support, Julian has gone on to become an inspirational speaker whose message touches people in all areas of their lives. She has spoken for various conferences and has won a speakers award. After listening to her message, one of her fans commented, 'It is because of you I did not give up on life'. She continues to work with people who are seeking to change their life's trajectory and rewrite their future. Indeed, Julian Businge is an example of a selfless humanitarian who is focused on helping people around the world achieve maximum success and live their best life. For more information, visit www.julianbusinge.com

Professor Patrick Businge, UK

Founder of Greatness University, Co-founder of The World Greatness Awards, Initiator of The World Greatness Day, Creator of The World Book of Greatness, Greatness Researcher, and Prolific Author

Born in Uganda, Professor Patrick Businge did not let his circumstances characterised by war and abject poverty become his standard. Following his dreams while believing that no condition was permanent, he took steps to raise above his circumstances and made greatness his benchmark.

Upon completing his PhD from Exeter, one of the world's finest universities, Professor Patrick Businge founded Greatness University in 2017. This is now the world's first and only institution dedicated to discovering, developing, delivering, and sustaining greatness in individuals and businesses. In order to help people tap into it faster than they could ever imagine, Professor Patrick Businge created the *World Greatness Awards* in 2019 that globally recognise and reward greatness; designated 15th August of each year as the *World Greatness Day* when greatness is internationally celebrated; and invented the *World Book of Greatness* which documents the legends, icons, leading lights, creators, finders, seekers, and masters of greatness from around the world.

Professor Patrick Businge has researched kings like the Omukama Oyo of Tooro: the World's Youngest Ruling Monarch as recorded in the Guinness Book of World Records. He has partnered with World Civility Leaders like His Excellency Dr Clyde Rivers, Ambassador at Large for Burundi and Founder of IChange Nations. He has researched celebrities like Les Brown, the World's Number 1 Motivational Speaker.

He has researched and branded businessmen like Antonio T Smith Jr, the CEO of ATS Group of Companies. He has also researched renowned church leaders in the UK like Archbishop Doye T Agama and churches likes The City of Refuge in Delaware, USA. He has advised African Queens, Princesses, Royal Ministers, and coached professionals and entrepreneurs on how to document their greatness and leave a legacy.

Professor Patrick Businge has written peer-reviewed journal articles, published over 12 books, and co-authored with over 200 people. Through his greatness coaching, mentoring and consultation; Professor Patrick Businge continues to help individuals, businesses, organisations, kingdoms, and nations reright their lives and rewrite their future. In this endeavour, iChange Nations has created an award titled: *The Professor Patrick Businge Greatness Award* which is given to people who have personally been mentored by him or emulated his example. Any donations linked to this award are dedicated to the education of children in Africa living in settings characterized by war and abject poverty similar to what he experienced when growing up.

Professor Patrick Businge holds international posts such as being a Representative to the United Nations where he speaks about peace and peacebuilding. He has also received an honorary doctorate from the United Graduate College and Seminary International. He is a Distinguished Fellow of the Order of St. Hadrian of Canterbury: a fellowship bestowed upon him by the Apostolic Pastoral Conference.

H.E Dr Clyde Rivers, USA

Founder & President of iChange Nations, World Civility Leader, Ambassador at Large for Burundi, Global Board Chairman of OPAD, and Global Spokesperson for the World Civility Day

His Excellency Dr. Clyde Rivers is the President and Founder of iChange Nations™. With its slogan "We Honor Ambassadors and Build Statesmen", iChange Nations is the largest "building cultures of honor" network in the world that recognises individuals who have exemplified extraordinary humanitarian efforts to positively change nations.

Dr Clyde Rivers is also the Spokesperson for the World Civility Day and Community Civility Counts Initiative. As a World Civility Leader and Peace Ambassador, Dr. Clyde Rivers believes that every life is valuable and has been created to bring a contribution to the world. Dr. Clyde Rivers uses the Golden Rule "Treat others the way you want to be treated" as his guiding principle in honouring what is good in humankind through *The Golden Rule International* and his organization, *iChange Nations*.

Dr Clyde Rivers has received awards, honours and held offices including being the:

- *Global Board Chairman to OPAD*
- Recipient of the Nelson Mandela International Peace Award 2019
- Representative to the United Nations – New York for the Interfaith Peace-Building Initiative (IPI) and the United Nations Department of Public Information (DPI)
- Representative to the United Nations for the Kenya Peace Society

Department of Ecosoc.

- Winning the Presidential Volunteer Service Award 2019
- Recipient of the Creativity United, "We Dream in Color," Humanitarian Icon of the Year Award 2018.

In 2017, Dr. Rivers won the United States Presidential Life Achievement Award for over 4,000 volunteer hours of serving the nation and humanity. He is also the recipient of the Danny K. Davis Peace Prize 2017, U.S. Congressman of Illinois. This annual Congressional Award given for excelling in his field and making a difference in people's lives.

In 2017, Dr. Rivers was given the Title of Don/Sir when he was Knighted into the original Kingdom of Guatemala and the great city of La Antigua: the first city established by the Spanish Monarchy. He was knighted by Lord EDUARDO L. PRADO S. the Commodore De Santiago De Los Caballeros De La Antigua Guatemala. Dr. Rivers is the recipient of an Honorable Mention for the American Civic Collaboration Award 2017 which celebrates partnerships that strengthen America.

Dr. Clyde Rivers is the Honorary Ambassador at Large for the Republic of Burundi, as appointed by H.E. President Pierre Nkurunziza and Special Advisor to President Pierre Nkurunziza, President of Republic of Burundi Africa.

Professors of Greatness

This honorary award is offered in conjunction with our partner *The United Graduate College and Seminary International* in the USA. It honours people who have gone where there is no path and created a trail.

These are the believers in greatness, the innovators, knowledge creators, global influencers, visionaries, leading lights, and paradigm creators who have immensely contributed to the world through their academic work, authorship and whose lived experience has created positive ripples in the world.

Archbishop Kiiza Thomas Sibayirwa, Uganda

Founder of Bwera University, Founder of Van Merode College of Applied Sciences & Technology, Founder of New Covenant Community School, and Leading Archbishop of The Ecumenical Orthodox- Catholic Church-EOCC

Dr. Thomas Kiiza is an academic, author, and missionary. He is always searching for knowledge and sharing it in conferences and symposiums. He is always creating new ideas and publishing them in books and academic journals. He is always reflecting on his experience and using it to positively impact the world.

Here are some of his major achievements and responsibilities in the past decade:

- 2017 to date: Founder of Bwera University, Uganda
- 2017 to date: Chairperson at African Ark College of Management, Uganda
- 2016-2018: Senior Lecturer, Mountains of the Moon University, Uganda
- 2013-2017: Academic Registrar, Mountains of the Moon University
- 2014-2015 Dean of Studies, Mountains of the Moon University, Uganda
- 2012 to date: Founder & Director, Van Merode College, Uganda
- 2013 to date: Founder, New Covenant Community School, Bwera, Uganda
- 2010-2013 Lecturer, The Catholic University of Eastern Africa, Kenya
- 2010-2014 Lecturer, St. James The Elder University, Florida, USA.

We have reviewed Dr Thomas Kiiza's accomplishments and he has served humanity well as a searcher of new information and a creator of new narratives. Greatness University in partnership with the United Graduate College and Seminary International consider it an honor and privilege to bestow upon him the prestigious Professorship Award and permit him to use the title of Professor.

Legends of Greatness

This prestigious award is bestowed to people who have globally replicated greatness and their legacy has been researched and documented by Greatness University. The Legend of Greatness Award completes the greatnisation process: the official declaration of a person as great and the inscription into the *World Book of Greatness.*

King Oyo Nyimba Kabamba Iguru Rukidi IV, Uganda

King of Tooro Kingdom in Uganda, United Nations Goodwill Ambassador, and The World's Youngest Ruling Monarch

www.kingoyo.africa

His Majesty Dr. Oyo Nyimba Kabamba Iguru Rukidi IV, the King of Tooro Kingdom in Uganda was born on 16th April 1992. When his father, Rukirabasaija Patrick David Matthew Rwamuhokya Kaboyo Olimi III passed away on 26th August 1995, the 3-year old Prince Oyo ascended to the throne on 12th September 1995, entering the Guinness Book of World Records as the Youngest Reigning Monarch.

Now aged 27 years, King Oyo has significant influence and respect among young people worldwide. He is leading initiatives to enable young people realize their potential and contribute positively to development of their communities and countries. His Majesty King Oyo is very passionate about agriculture and entrepreneurship. In October 2016, he started the "Agriculture is Wealth" initiative that inspires the youth to engage in agriculture or farming as a business for wealth creation, solving unemployment and establishing food and income security. King Oyo is also setting up model farms; and establishing partnerships for agriculture modernization, knowledge and technology transfer, research, climate change mitigation, and adaptation and market access.

His Majesty King Oyo has also established the "King Oyo Youth Innovations Fund" to inspire and support the youth to develop innovations and solutions to some of today's greatest challenges like ending the HIV/AIDS epidemic, addressing unemployment, eradicating poverty, ensuring food security, managing disasters and promoting culture.

His Majesty King Oyo was appointed a United Nations Goodwill Ambassador for ending HIV/AIDS among the youth by 2030 because of his personal commitment in the fight against HIV/AIDS and his continued efforts for meaningful involvement of youth and cultural leaders in ending the AIDS epidemic. As UNAIDS Goodwill Ambassador, King Oyo is engaging and inspiring over 500 million young people to take a stand against HIV/AIDS using a creative mix of youth innovations, edutainment, sports, social media and advocacy.

In 2014, King Oyo was awarded an Honorary Doctorate of Peace by the University of Vietnam for his great work in fostering peace and reconciliation. He is also a recipient of the World Civility Award from iChange Nations for exemplifying extraordinary humanitarian efforts to effectively change the his kingdom. He has a degree in Business Administration from the University of Winchester in the UK and has received other academic honours.

Our research indicates that King Oyo has globally replicated greatness and is creating a legacy. This world is documented in his upcoming biography researched by Greatness University. We at Greatness University are honoured to recognise him as a *Legend of Greatness.*

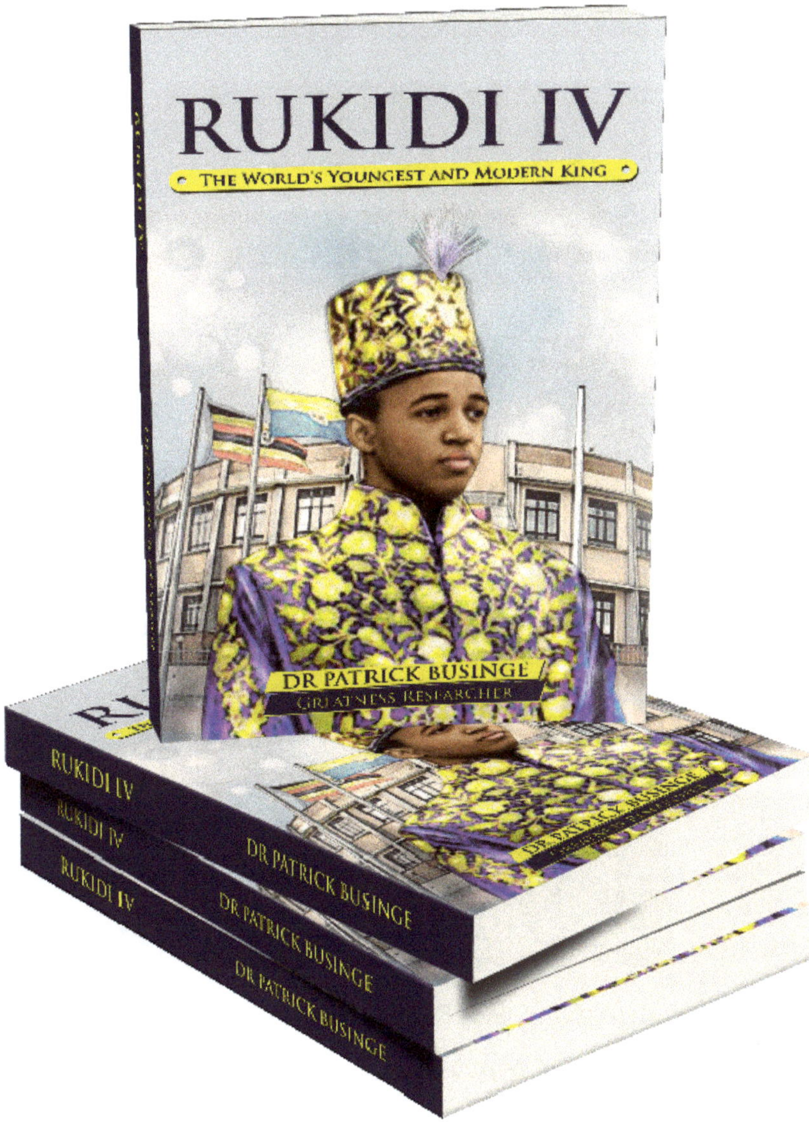
RUKIDI IV
THE WORLD'S YOUNGEST AND MODERN KING
DR PATRICK BUSINGE
GREATNESS RESEARCHER
RUKIDI IV
DR PATRICK BUSINGE
RUKIDI IV
DR PATRICK BUSINGE
RUKIDI IV
DR PATRICK BUSINGE

Archbishop Doye T Agama, UK

Presiding Prelate of the Apostolic Pastoral Congress, Leader of the 'Christian Way of Life' Group of Churches, Prominent Figure in the 'Churches Together in England', and Author of the Series 'African Christianity and the Bible'

Born in Shirley, Southampton, England in the mid-1950s, Archbishop Doyé Agama was fostered early as a baby in London. He re-joined his natural family in Nigeria in the early 1960's and only returned to England after the civil war occasioned by the attempted secession of "Biafra".

With royal lineages on both sides of his natural heritage, Archbishop Doyé Agama's father was His Royal Highness, Chief Frederick Abiye Agama, the Ogbotom Edede of the Epie-Atissa Clan in Bayelsa State of Nigeria. His maternal grandfather, Chief Nelson Kemeninabokide Porbeni, was the Etonkepua of Kabowei Kingdom, and the Ododomedo of Asideni in Delta State of Nigeria. Bishop's mother, HRH Chief Beatrice Agama (nee Porbeni) arrived in England with his father in 1953, where they were both studying in higher education. Late King Frederick Agama was a witness of some of the early evangelization of the Niger Delta and a pioneer in the origin Niger Delta Diocese of the Church of Nigeria.

A man of many parts, the Most Reverend Doyé Agama is a former Telecommunications Consultant to the Oil Industry, Central and Local Government and the Emergency Services. He first started work as a teaching assistant in 1973, and has also been involved at various times in Community Development and Regeneration work since 1975. He is a PRINCE2 Practitioner and Business Analyst, with a practice background in Strategic, Program, Project, Operational Technical and Financial Business Intelligence. A former journalist, documentary film-maker, dramatist and jazz impresario, he also has over twenty years of very wide experience in the offshore oil industry, the UK Public and Charity Sectors, including: Project Management and Consultancy in Data Infrastructure, IT System Engineering, Network Administration, Training and Staff Development.

Archbishop Doyé has participated in Bid Management, Technical and Operational Studies, Requirements Assessment and Gap Analysis Reports, Best Value Reviews, Strategy Reviews, Risk Assessments, Business Process Re-engineering and Business Case Development. His involvements have often covered the full program/project life cycle. The technologies Doyé has specialised in have included a variety of data networks, as well as landline and mobile telephony, HF, VHF, UHF, microwave point-to-point, satellite systems, sonar and radar. Doyé has held Certificates in Microsoft and Cisco Networking Technologies etc. He was also a consultant in the transition to Airwave for one of the largest UK Polices Forces.

The organisations he has worked for in the past include: The Post Office, Thames Valley Police, the Department of Works and Pensions, Community Service Volunteers, the College of Venereal Disease Prevention, Wigan MBC, Liverpool City Council, Praxis-HIS Consulting Limited, Mason Communications, Durham City Council, Telford and Wrekin Council, British Nuclear Fuels, CAMCO, WASCO-OILTOOLS, First Aluminium, MAERSK Lines, Single Buoy Moorings, Air Liquide, SEACOR Global Santa Fé and Nowcam etc. He has also worked at local and regional levels for some of the biggest charities in the United Kingdom, including NACRO and Community Service Volunteers.

Coming to clergy ministry late in life, he was first ordained in 2004 and became a Pentecostal Bishop just ten years later. He is frequently called upon by Churches, Charities, Central and Local Government, the Emergency Services and other organisations in the United Kingdom for advice (and training) on community relations. He also aims to bring Christian (and other Religious Leaders) together with Civic and Business Leaders, for community benefit.

He is a former Member of the Council of Manchester Cathedral and Director and Trustee of the Ecumenical Council for Corporate Responsibility, ECCR (2009 till 2011) an Associate Member of the UK Restorative Justice Council and a Member of the Centre for Crime and Justice Studies. He served four years as a member of the Valuations Tribunal (2008-2012). He also served for several years as a Forcewide Chaplain to Greater Manchester Police Force, and is a former Member of GMP Independent Advisory Group, North Manchester Division. He has worked across the North of England to help resettle former prison inmates and he has as also run innovative alternative education for "NEET" students, those otherwise not in employment, education or training.

He has attended various Middle Level and Senior Management courses over the past 30 years. He has been a member of the British Computer Society, British

Institute of Public Sector Management etc. He has also been a member of The Institute of Electrical and Electronics Engineers, Chatham House (The Royal Institute of International Affairs), and is an Alumni of the Experienced Strategic Leaders Programme of the Windsor Leadership Trust held at Windsor Castle (Spring 2011).

Archbishop Doyé is an Alumni of the Cranfield University School of Management. He completed a two-year Certificate in Orthodox Theology with the Institute for Orthodox Theological Studies in Cambridge UK, in addition, to his earlier the BA Theology (Church Admin & Dev) 1994, and MA (Pastoral Counselling) 1996 from Ramona, California. He has been honoured with Doctoral Degrees (Honoraris Causa) Doctor of Letters from Academia del Fiorino, Florencia, Italy and Doctor of Divinity from the Joint College of African American Pentecostal Bishops, USA.

He is also a member of several Christian and cultural charities including the: Order of the Star of Ethiopia (Knight Grand Cross); Military & Hospitaller Order of St Lazarus of Jerusalem (Ecclesiastical Commander); and the Noble Communion and Holy Apostolic Order of St Hadrian of Canterbury (Knight Grand Cross and Abbot General). For more information, read the anthology that led to his greatnisation below titled Archbishop Doye T. Agama Changed Our Lives.

ARCHBISHOP
DOYÉ T. AGAMA
CHANGED OUR LIVES
Stories to Inspire You Respond to Your Calling
DR PATRICK BUSINGE
GREATNESS RESEARCHER

Professor Simeon Kayiwa, Uganda

Founder & Chancellor of Kayiwa International University, Founding Pastor of Namirembe Christian Fellowship, Gospel Singer, and Father of Born Again Christianity in Uganda

Professor Simeon Kayiwa is a Pastor, Academic and a renowned Gospel Singer. In December 1977, the Lord appeared to him and asked him to wake up and read Isaiah 60. What followed was the calling to start a ministry of healing that eventually led him to be the founding pastor of *Namirembe Christian Fellowship* in Uganda's capital Kampala. Writing a Foreword for his book *Walking on Miracles*, Tony Morton of the Cornerstone Network in Southampton, UK wrote: 'Simeon Kayiwa is a bright light shining in the universe of complex and fallen mankind... He is a man of revelation and conviction, who has lived faith, experienced the heavenlies, and has seen God's power to let loose on earth'. Today, Pastor Simeon Kayiwa ministers his flock through word and music. He is the Chairman of the *National Foundation of Born Again Churches* in Uganda. He is perceived by historians as the father of Born Again Christianity in Uganda.

Professor Simeon Kayiwa holds a Doctor of Philosophy (PhD) and a Doctor of Divinity from the Latin University of Theology, USA. He has researched the supernatural and mastered it in his thesis *The Supernatural Unfolded.* To his congregation, he is known as the *Miracle Man* and his upcoming anthology is filled with testimonies of miracles including those of raising people from the dead.

Professor Simeon Kayiwa is also the Founder and Chancellor of Kayiwa International University in Uganda. Writing a Foreword for the upcoming anthology titled *Simeon Kayiwa Changed Our Lives: Stories to Inspire You Escape to Triumph*, the World Civility Leader Professor Dr Clyde Rivers wrote, 'Kayiwa

International University will be known around the world as the home of supernatural literacy education originating from Uganda to the rest of the world'. Amongst his peers, Professor Simeon Kayiwa is the *Father of Supernatural Literacy* because of being the founder of this new paradigm of learning. Here at Greatness University, Professor Simeon Kayiwa is a *Legend of Greatness*. For more information read this anthology below that led to his greatnisation.

Archbishop Kiiza Thomas Sibayirwa, Uganda

Founder of Bwera University, Founder of Van Merode College of Applied Sciences & Technology, Founder of New Covenant Community School, and Leading Archbishop of The Ecumenical Orthodox- Catholic Church-EOCC

Archbishop Kiiza Thomas Sibayirwa, was born in 1976 and raised in the little village of Kisebere in Nyabugando Ward of Kasese District in Uganda. He went to Kamukumbi Rural Primary School from where he exhibited a high level of academic excellence. The little rural boy Kiiza joined St. Mary's Virika Seminary in Fort Portal where he excelled academically and went abroad for studies as a missionary student. Archbishop Kiiza holds four Degrees: a PhD (Doctorate) in Religious Studies & Theology, Master of Arts in Religious Studies, B.A (Hons) in Religious Studies & Theology of The Catholic University of Eastern Africa-Kenya, and B.A in Philosophy of The Pontifical Urbaniana University, Italy.

Bishop Kiiza is a fully trained Catholic Missionary and has served in different countries and organizations. He has recently been elected as The International Leading Bishop of The Ecumenical Orthodox- Catholic Church-EOCC. Dr. Kiiza Sibayirwa is a social entrepreneur and philanthropist. He is the CEO of EKisande African Communities Empowerment Initiatives, EKisande Rural Development Centre and a number of other successful grassroots community empowerment projects. He is a Distinguished Fellow of The Order St. Hadrian of Canterbury, UK.

Bishop Kiiza is the Charter (Founding) President of The Rotary Club of Fort Portal. He is the Author of *The Role of Christian Forgiveness in Restorative Justice and Reconciliation: A Response to Negative Ethnicity in African Societies.* He is also a motivational speaker and inspirational preacher. He has spoken at conferences in England (UK), Europe, Canada, USA, India, and Africa.

Research done by Greatness University indicates that Bishop Kiiza is person who is humble, simple and likes keeping a low but dignified profile. He is the uncelebrated celebrity, an agent of global peace and a blessing to humanity. He is happily married to his Queen Mrs. Reena Biira Kiiza and they have three (3) lovely children. For more information, read the anthology below.

Mr Antonio T Smith Jr, USA

Founder of ATS Business University, Best-selling author, Popular Podcast Host Successful Businessman, and Prolific Public Speaker

Antonio T. Smith, Jr. is a prolific public speaker certified by Les Brown, the world's greatest motivational speaker, who has delivered over 2000 keynotes at events such as the University of Houston, Wiley College, which you can listen to on his podcast. Antonio is an internationally recognized trainer and speaker, and best-selling author in self-help and religious categories. He specializes in Cognitive Behavior Therapy, Business and Strength Training, Leadership, Teleconference Presentations, Personal Breakthroughs, Prosperity Consciousness, Mindset Training, and all levels of effective marketing. Antonio also owns one of the most successful technology companies in Texas. He holds a Bachelors degree in Christianity and a Masters in Theological Studies.

Antonio T. Smith, Jr. is a best-selling author and a popular podcast host with a show that reaches over 70 countries and 60 different languages. He has been coaching people around the world on personal transformation for the last 9 years and reaches over hundreds of thousands of listeners across the globe.

Antonio overcame abandonment, homelessness, and brokenness. He had to learn at the tender age of six how to use his mind to climb out of sleeping in a dumpster. He would spend his entire childhood homeless, was adopted when he was 14, and aged out of CPS custody at 18 years old. This Galveston, TX native has been through more in his 30+ years than most will ever experience. He has developed a "plant better" attitude, in which he teaches people to plant better seeds in order to have a better life. Antonio has developed coaching tools, programs, courses and books designed to help the world succeed. Today he is a certified Les Brown Partner, a renown public speaker, and leadership coach.

Antonio Smith Jr. graduated from the Houston Baptist University twice. First, with his Bachelors of Arts in Christianity; and second, with his Masters of Arts in Theological Studies. Antonio T. Smith Jr has served as pastor of a small Baptist church in Galveston, Texas and is one of the most sought after preachers in South East Texas. Based on his rich academic and business experience, he founded ATS Business University and travels the world giving lectures.

According to our research Antonio T Smith Jr is an angel, a giver, mentor, king, and soldier. According to his people, Antonio gives them clarity, gratitude, encouragement. He is a symbol of success and possibility. Our research confirms that Antonio T Smith Jr has globally replicated greatness and is creating a legacy. We at Greatness University are honoured to recognise him as a *Legend of Greatness*. For more information read the anthology titled *Antonio T Smith Jr Changed Our Lives* below that led to his greatnisation.

FOREWORD BY Les Brown, World's Greatest Motivational Speaker & Serena Brown Travis, The Pulpit Chic
Antonio T. Smith Jr.
CHANGED OUR LIVES
Stories To Inspire You To Plant Better
DR PATRICK BUSINGE
Celebrity Researcher

Icons of Greatness

The Icon of Greatness Award is given to people who through their initiatives, businesses, and charities, have served humanity well and are living examples of selfless service.

Sultan Siddig Adam Abdalla Elhaj, Sudan

Famously known as Sideeg Wada'a

Siddeeg Adam Abdalla Elhaj famously known as Siddeeg Wada'a is the Sultan of Sudan. He has received accolades due to his tireless efforts to making the lives of people in Sudan better. Here is a summary of his accolades and contributions.

Orders and Accolades:

- The Order of Sudan's Loyal Son by President of the Republic in appreciation to his contributions to public activities
- Honorary Doctorate from the University of El Fashir, Sudan
- Honorary Doctorate from the University of West Kordofan, Sudan

Public and Private Sector Posts assumed which reflect his national contributions:

- In the Field of Administration and Governance: Member of El Fasher District Council 1983; Member of the National Council (the Parliament) in several previous terms; Member of the current National Council (2015/2020) representing a constituency which includes Umkadada, Dar Asalam and Klaimando; and Member of the Consultative Council of the National Congress Party.

- In the field of Peace Building: President of the committee nominated to contact the non-signatory armed factions in Doha Document for Peace in Darfur (DDPD); President of the Internal Darfur/Darfur Dialogue and Consultation Committee; Deputy Chairperson of Um Jaras Initiative; and the custodian of Peace talks between the Government of Sudan and Justice and the Equality Movement (JEM) in 2004.

- In the Field of Humanitarian and Charitable works: President of the Board of Directors of Klaimando Development Organization and President of the Council of Custodians of Tabarak Charitable Organization.
- In the Field of Business and Financial Activities: President of the Board of Directors of the Export Development Bank; A key shareholder of El Mashreq Bank; and Founder and President of the Board of Directors of Sidgo Group of Companies which is comprcised of more than 15 companies.
- In the Field of High Education: Member of the Board of Directors of the University of Khartoum: Member of the Senate of the University of Bahry; Member of the Senate of the University of Al Fasher; Member of the Senate of Al Easher Technical College; Deputy President of the Council of the Custodians of Klaimendo Community Development College.
- In the Field of Media and Culture: President of the Board of Directors of Al Akhbar Multi-activity Company and the owner of Al Akhbar Newspaper and President of the Board of Directors of Klaimando Cultural Centre.

Initiatives and Participations in the National Efforts:

- Darfur Peace Building where he was the initiator and first Sudanese ever to mediate between the government and the armed opposition in regional and international forums.
- Kinana Conference on the unification of Sudanese vision on national issues.
- Humanitarian and charitable field where he constructed mosques in Sudan and abroad and has funded 40 pilgrims to Mecca for the past 10 years.
- Facilitated reconciliation between various tribes in Darfur
- Contributions to Education where he constructed a five-story building to be used as lecture halls and study rooms at the University of Khartoum; construction of the lecture hall at Al Fashir University; construction of the computer sciences and lecture hall at the University of West Kordofan; a donation for the construction of the Faculty of Computer Sciences and a lecture hall in the University of Al Di'ain in East Darfur; construction of the Faculty of Haj Siddeeg Wada'a in Klaimendo; constructed all the Basic and Secondary Schools in Klaimendo Locality; Constructed a Basic School in Mongula, South Sudan; Fully maintained the Sudanese School in Ndjamena, Tchad; Constructed a number of residential compounds with the appropriate educational environment for the girl students; Maintained all the basic schools in Wada'a and the neighboring villages; construction of Al Timaid high Secondary school In Armal , West Kordufan.

Water Harvesting Projects:

- Drilling 25 artesian wells basically in Klaimendo locality and other areas in North Darfur
- Constructed the damp of Um Shaggag across Wadi Al Kou', North Darfur
- Constructed the damp of Wad Koata , North Darfur

Construction and Maintenance of Mosques:

- Construction of mosques in each of Klaimendo, Um baitain, Gossa Jammat, Sania Karaou, Wad Koata, Bahar Omdorman (North Darfur), Al Siraiha (wad Madani, Al Jazeera), Dilaig (Central Darfur). Bila il (south Darfur), North Omdurman (Khartoum State)
- The maintenance of the mosque of Wau, South Sudan

Health Care:

- Construction of a 60-bed-capacity hospital in Klaimendo
- Construction of a big ward in the Hospital of the Hot Climate Diseases in Omdurman
- Construction of a ward in Al Fashir hospital (North Darfur)
- Construction of a ward in Nyala hospital (South Darfur)
- Construction of a 60-bed-capacity hospital in Wada'a, North Darfur
- Construction of an obstetrics and genecology section in Al dia'in hospital

Sports and Recreation:

- The support of leading football clubs in Sudan (Hilal, Mirrikh).
- Support of the leading football clubs in North Darfur (Hilal, Mirrikh)
- Support of a number of football clubs all around the Sudan
- The Support of the equestrian clubs by offering them a number of hi-bred horses with the objective of raising the quality of horses in the Sudan
- Haj Siddeeg has as a big concern the agriculture (animals and plants), wildlife and environment.
- He has as a hobby the equestrianism and the breeding of hi-bred horses. He owns, in fact, the biggest stable in the Sudan.

We at Greatness University have reviewed his accomplishments and it is evident that he has stepped into his greatness and positively changed the Sudan. We therefore consider it an honour to bestow upon him the prestigious World Greatness Award. As Sultan Siddig Adam Abdalla Elhaj Roach has served humanity and is a living example of selfless service, we recognise him as worthy of the title *Icon of Greatness.*

Queen Best Kemigisa, Uganda

Queen Mother, Humanitarian, and Educator

www.hakyooto.com

Queen Best Kemigisa of Tooro Kingdom in Uganda was born in 1967. She is mother to King Oyo Nyimba Kabamba Iguru Rukidi IV, the reigning Omukama of Tooro. She is the daughter of Prince Mujunju of the Batuku clan of Rwebisengo, Bundibugyo District. She was educated at Kahinju Primary School, Mpanga Senior Secondary School and Kyebambe Girls School, all in the Kingdom of Tooro.

Queen Best Kemigisa is the Founder and Patron of *Tooro Women's Development Association, African Kings Forum* and a co-founder of *African Queens and Women Cultural Leaders Network*. Queen Best Kemigisa is passionate about issues that affect girls, women and children in Africa. Most of her work takes place through the *Queen Mother Best Foundation (QMBF)*: a registered NGO located in Tooro Kingdom, Uganda. Since its inception, the QMBF acts as a platform for the promotion of human rights, HIV awareness, hygiene and sanitation, primary education, vocational and life skills development.

Queen Best Kemigisa uses HAKYOOTO as a vehicle to achieve her aims and objectives. A Rutooro word meaning 'around the bonfire', Hakyooto is organised in various parts of Tooro Kingdom and African countries. Hakyooto events involve coming together so as to listen and learn through storytelling, music, dance and drama as means to educate people about their culture. Various influencers are interviewed and harmful practices are symbolically burnt on the bonfire so that people are able to re-right their future.

Queen Best Kemigisa welcomes all well-intentioned people and organisations to team up with her in realising her mission of educating, entertaining and empowering the people of Tooro and Africa. For more information, visit www.hakyooto.com As Queen Best Kemigisa has consistently engaged in positive action which has transformed the world, we recognise her as worthy the title *Icon of Greatness.*

Mr Ty Cohen, USA

Internet Marketer, Radio Personality, Author, and King of Kindle

www.tycohen.com

Ty Cohen is an accomplished internet marketer, and former morning talk show radio personality (WCLY 1150 Raleigh, NC). He is an author and creator of over a dozen best-selling books, software programs, directories and products. Over the last 11 years, Ty Cohen has taught thousands of individuals how to successfully market, promote and sell their products and services online.

Ty has a simple formula for turning life's obstacles into life's financial opportunities that enable people to effectively reach their personal and/or business goals. Using a unique combination of tested and proven methods and resources, Ty's goal is to educate and empower people with the tools needed to operate a successful business both online and offline. His message has taken him to many places in the United States and the around the world such as Thailand, Singapore, Malaysia, and New Zealand. For more information, visit www.tycohen.com

We at Greatness University have reviewed Ty Cohen's accomplishments and it is evident that he has stepped into his greatness and positively changed the world. We therefore consider it an honour to bestow upon him Icon of Greatness Award.

Mr Julian Hall, UK

Ultrapreneur, Author and Humanitarian

www.julianhall.co.uk

Featured in Forbes, 'The Ultrapreneur' Julian Hall is the founder of a four year old social enterprise called *Ultra Education* which has been successfully teaching entrepreneurship to primary and secondary school aged children from disadvantaged backgrounds in the United Kingdom. The multi award winning organisation's mission is to provide all children and young people, regardless of background or social standing, with access to effective entrepreneurial education.

Based on his background in technology and investment banking, Julian Hall is the bestselling author of three business books. He has also co-written 3 degrees in entrepreneurship and launched the UK's first mobile game for kids entrepreneurship. A recently elected member of the Guild of Entrepreneurs and freeman of the city, Julian is currently developing the world's first artificial intelligence chatbot that can also teach entrepreneurship to kids and teens. Julian Hall was a winner of London Prestige Awards, National Mentee of the Year, Pride of Brent SME of the Year and finalist on the National Business Awards. For more information, visit https://julianhall.co.uk

As Julian Hall has served humanity and is a living example of selfless service, we at Greatness University recognise him as worthy of the title *Icon of Greatness.*

Dr Robin Lococo, USA

Founder of Challenged Champions and Heroes, Board Member of iChange Nations, and International Ambassador for the Golden Rule

Dr Robin Lococo is the Founder of Challenged Champions and Heroes: an organization that brings honor and recognition to the physically and mentally challenged people of the world. Being a Challenged Champion herself, Dr Robin Lococo, understands what it is like to be treated differently because of physical disabilities. This has never stopped her in achieving her dreams. Dr Robin Lococo uses an awareness campaign which showcases that every "Life is Valuable". She also facilitates education models in over 80 countries including the United States, Uganda, Kenya, Ivory Coast, Nigeria and the United Arab Emirates.

Dr Robin Lococo holds various educational qualifications including:

- Bachelor of Theology, Latin University of Theology, Inglewood, CA, 2009
- Master of Divinity, United Graduate College and Seminary, NC, 2010
- Doctorate in Christian Counseling, United Graduate College and Seminary, Mars Hills, NC, 2010
- Doctorate of Society and Human Rights, Latin University of Theology, 2014

Dr Robin Lococo also holds international appointments that include being the:

- Executive Director North America Division of IPI-Interfaith Peace-Building Initiative (Golden Rule) Addis Ababa, Ethiopia
- Board Member of iChange Nations and Executive Director of Administration
- International Ambassador for the Golden Rule
- Special Projects Coordinator to Amb. Clyde Rivers for Burundi, Africa

- Executive Director of Administration for iChange Nations
- Global Director of Media for IChange Nations
- UN NGO Representative for the Peace Society of Kenya.

Due to her dedication, Dr Robin Lococo has received various awards such as:

- The 2017 United States Presidential lifetime achievement award for doing over 4000 hours of volunteer services and aid to the great people of the United States of America
- Top 20 Global Woman of Excellence Recognition Award on March 9, 2018: a Congressional Award given at the International Woman's Day Celebration presented by U.S. Congressman Danny K. Davis 7th Congressional District-Il and the Multi Ethnic Advisory Task Force (MEATF)
- Ambassador for Peace Award from the Universal Peace Federation which is recognized in 154 nations.

As Dr Robin Lococo has consistently engaged in positive action which has transformed the world, we at Greatness University recognise her as worthy the title *Icon of Greatness.*

Professor Ona C. Miller, USA

Founder of First Ladies Global Institute™, Female Civility Icon,
Goodwill Ambassador for the Golden Rule, and
Creator of Nation Female Civility Day

Professor Ona C. Miller is an international professor and a qualitative researcher that has extended previous studies in the secular universities, but has expanded her expertise in the sacred faith-based universities as a strategic educator that searches to create and author curriculum to change the female perception and position of women globally. Professor Ona has a Doctorate of Professorship (PhD) from United Graduate College and Seminary International and a Doctorate in Organizational Leadership (EdD). Her expertise is in "Resolving Issues by searching reasons of behaviors with Women as it pertains to Female Civility, Women in Leadership, Global Relations, and Organizational and Structural Leadership."

Professor Ona has served as a panelist on "The Role that Civility and Leadership in Social Protection at the United Nations Commission on the Status of Women" (CSW63). She has collected and continues to seek data to identify the internal and external barriers that exist for women because of social, economic, cultural, and traditional barriers, while implementing strategies for women to overcome.

Professor Ona is an appointed representative for the Advancement of Women and Girls with the Peace Society of Kenya, which is a non-governmental organization with consultative status with the United Nations Economic and Social Council. She is a founding member on the Board of Directors for *YOU! Empower.* a non-profit organization designed to provide disadvantage women and families with the tools and resources to empower themselves towards a self-sustainable lifestyle. She is also an advocate for women and an authorized Civility Spokesperson with the

Civility Speakers Bureau and the author of motivational books, workbooks, and case studies to help women gain confidence, equality, advancement, and stability.

Professor Ona is appointed and commissioned by the Interfaith Peace-Building Initiative as a Goodwill Ambassador for the Golden Rule and is an International World Civility Ambassador. She has been awarded the Women of Global Solutions Award and the Golden Rule International Award by the iChange Nations™ Organization supported by the United Nations.

Professor Ona is the Female Civility Icon and has founded a Nation Female Civility Day that is celebrate globally every year. Female Civility is a global culture of RESPECT that values the creative and unique existence of FEMALES worldwide. Female Civility eradicates preset stigmas and judgments that were established by an unlearned traditional society. Female Civility enhances the quality of every FEMALE in every nation. Female Civility breaks generational barriers to create and activate a new narrative through education, by embracing femininity and revealing an identity of authenticity. Every FEMALE is valued and their PURPOSE and LEGACY will be established.

As the founder of First Ladies Global Institute™: an online platform to build and ignite women in leadership to embrace who they are ashamedly, Professor Ona is also the founder of the iPreneuse™ Movement: an international, interracial, and intercultural movement designed to provide solutions to the economic and educational disadvantaged women around the world. Included in Professor Ona's mission is WombHER Foundation for antiabortion and anti-abandonment for women. Women must stop aborting and abandoning their purpose and identity. Professor Ona also served as the former National Economic Director and Legislative Adviser for the United States Women Christian Chamber of Commerce. She has also been awarded the CFO Award for Superior Mission Achievement Comptroller Award by the Department of Homeland Security.

As an author, Professor Ona has written several books including: "I Am Single, 8 Elements for Implementing Your Purpose, 8 Elements for Implementing Your Purpose Workbook, and Supplements for Life's Deficiencies, Christian Ministry Leaders: The Barriers that Women Face in Non-Profit Organizations, Civility and Womanhood: Women embracing empathizing and Empowering Women, and Female Civility in Leadership". As Professor Ona C Miller has served humanity and is a living example of selfless service, we recognise her as worthy of the title *Icon of Greatness.*

Dr Ira Roach III, Delaware, USA

Founder of The City of Refuge, Award-winning Actor, and Author

Dr Ira Roach III holds a Bachelors degree in counseling, Masters degree in Christian Education and Doctorate in Christian Education and Organizational Leadership & Development. He has been pinned by many as the "Motivator to the Masses" with his many years of experience as a spiritual leader speaking to audiences in Delaware, Maryland, Virginia, New Jersey and Pennsylvania.

Dr Ira Roach III is an award-winning actor in the web series Church Folk Secrets, an international bestselling author, certified trainer, speaker and coach. He also hosts a weekly online show *Journey 2 Success* which highlights entrepreneurs, professionals, leaders, artists and dreamers. He has a passion for helping people with tools to change the quality of their lives in the religious arena and self-help industry. He specializes in "Getting Unstuck" (mindset mastery training), Leadership and Personal development, Workforce/job readiness training, team building and "What's Your Story?" (Story development, Writing a book).

Dr Ira Roach III saw his parents divorced at the age 4 and developed a mentality of blame and guilt, "it's my fault." Years of carrying around unnecessary guilt led him down a journey of brokenness, depression, low self-esteem and most of all a poverty-stricken (small) mindset. Years of being stuck and not knowing how to get "unstuck," his life from 26-40 years old had lows. His low self-confidence affected relationships, creativity and he finally struck his version of rock bottom. He was divorced after 14 years, faced public humiliation and three failed attempts of being an entrepreneur. His breakthrough came after he enlisted the help of a counselor and discovered his "breakthrough". In 2017, his life changed when he understood what his gift was to the world. Dr Ira hopes to add value and help millions of people who don't know where to start. He has adopted a popular saying that his mentor gave him: "from small town to big stage!"

We at Greatness University have reviewed his accomplishments and it is evident that he has stepped into his greatness and positively changed the world. We therefore consider it an honour to bestow upon him the prestigious World Greatness Award. As Dr Ira Roach III has served humanity and is a living example of selfless service, we recognise him as worthy of the title *Icon of Greatness.*

Dr Jason Renville, USA

Founder & CEO of Jason Renville International, Empowerment Facilitator, TV Host, Co-Founder of Goshen Safe Haven Community Development Center (GSHCDC)

www.iamjasonrenville.com

Dr. Jason Renville is not only the prolific author of "Bring My Soul Out of Prison"- Revive, Renew and Restore the Mind, and Embracing Your Mark of Authenticity- A creed to Humanity but a sought-after empowerment facilitator: television host, a consultant, teacher, and a life coach in the areas of personal development, individual excellence, leadership and human development. Dr. Renville is widely regarded in the ecclesiastical, corporate and government agencies and Human Development market as one of the most prolific facilitators in the fields of peak performance, personal and organizational building and success. His enthusiasm, sense of humor, and refreshing perspectives on "The Authentic You "and "psychological and sustainable leadership" have delighted and enlightened international and mainstream audiences in the United States.

Renville arrived in the US in 2002, in pursuit of continuing his professional studies, and with a few hundred dollars and a bag full of dreams from Guyana, South America. His accomplishments are a great example of the entrepreneurial spirit that so characterizes the fact that with a relentless focus and unwavering determination, one can accomplish the IMPOSSIBLE.

Through in-house workshops on leadership and human development, to life-changing events for hundreds of people, and having the awesome opportunity to have counseled and advised people from every walk of life, from "Major Organization" executives to educators, entrepreneurs, community, pastors, students, and business leaders. He has been featured on local and nationally syndicated television and radio such as TCT and *Trinity Broadcasting Network* several times (TBN), and *The Word Network* which are seen and heard worldwide, where he also appears as a regular host for programs where he presents his revelations, insights, philosophy and practical guidance on how to achieve one's personal best and create well-balanced Authentic and dynamic life through utilizing time –tested leadership, governance and human development principles.

Dr. Renville is the CEO and founder of Jason Renville International, and is also the co-founder along with his wife Jenny of the Goshen Safe Haven Community Development Center for Development - Education and Empowerment (GSHCDC), an organization whose mission is to empower the community with the personal and professional development tools and strategies to achieve their personal dreams and become successful role models to future generations.

His research in Strategic Organizational Leadership, Human Development, and Governmental Studies has led him to dialogue about leadership, authenticity, human relations, women's empowerment social reconstruction, economic development, mental health and a host of other humanitarian issues.

Dr. Renville also serves as Human Rights Representative to the United Nations as well as Global Ambassador -At -Large and Ecclesiastical Officer with the same organization (UN) under the economic and social counsel (NGO). Additionally, Dr. Renville is the Leadership and certifying Agent for the President's Volunteer

Service Award program in the US, Senior Global Director of Leadership, Governance and Human Development of OPAD Organization for Poverty Alleviation and Development - UN/USA, Asia, Latin America &the Caribbean, Ecclesiastical and Governance Counselor & Executive Board Member of Phoenix Corporation for Global Development and Educational Representative of United Gradate College & Seminary International.

He matriculated from institutions such as the University of Guyana and Bentley Coaching Institute and Kingdom University amongst other leading schools in the US. He is also a recipient of several honorary doctorates from Universities with the US. Also, earned doctorate -PhD from Florida Theological University, with a concentration on Organizational Leadership, Human Development and Governmental Studies. Despite all these accomplishments, when asked if he regards himself as an author, speaker, entrepreneur or academician,

Dr. Renville prefers to think of himself as both a coach and a cheerleader to those want to become architects of their own authenticity. His work in support of the education and leadership of both the corporate and church communities has been recognized by many organizations. He has been a recipient of the following:

- Nelson Mandela International Peace Award 2019
- iChange Nations' World Civility Award -2018
- iChange Nations' Peace Icon Award – Diplomat of The Year – 2019.

Dr Farookh Sensei, India

8 World Records Holder, International Leadership Master Trainer, National Karate Champion, International Best Selling Author, Speaker & Empowerment Coach

www.farookhsensei.com

Dr Farookh Sensei has made various transitions in life. From a school dropout to a World Record holder in international aviation studies with 41 IATA qualifications. From a back-bencher to a John Maxwell & Les Brown licensed international leadership master trainer, speaker & empowerment Coach to conduct training in 48 countries worldwide. From the poorest performer in the class to 4 times national karate champion of India, and Asian brand Ambassador to represent two World Karate Championships in Brazil and Italy. From an unfit pilot trainee to a 5 Star Airline Instructor to train experienced pilots including Captains flying Super Jumbo Airbus A380s. From a terrible writer to Amazon International Best Selling Author.

Dr Farookh Sensei is World Record holder for 18 years for having achieved 41 IATA (Airline) qualifications. He broke his own World Record 8 times in 18 years and obtained a Doctorate from the World Records University (UK). He is a Certified Coach, Teacher and Speaker with John Maxwell (No.1 Leadership Expert in the World) and with Les Brown (No. 1 Motivational Expert in the World). He has conducted training in more than 48 Countries. He is an Author, Entrepreneur, Keynote Speaker, Transformation and Leadership Coach, Learning and Performance Specialist, and an NLP Master Practitioner.

Dr Farookh Sensei is the Director of Honeydew Group; Chief Leadership Director of Happy Genius CEO easy D.G (online dangerous goods training provider for airlines); President & CEO of ISKKA'89 (International Shotokan Karate Kodokai

Association); CEO K3 'Fight for Bike'. He has also represented Qatar in 2 World Karate Championships in Brazil & Italy. For more information, visit www.farookhsensei.com

We at Greatness University have reviewed his accomplishments and it is evident that he has stepped into his greatness and positively changed the world. We therefore consider it an honour to bestow upon him the prestigious World Greatness Award. As Dr Farookh Sensei has served humanity and is a living example of selfless service, we recognise him as worthy of the title *Icon of Greatness.*

Professor Jacob Simon George, India

Founder & Chancellor of Good News International University

www.goodnewsuniversity.org

Born in the city of Chennai in India, Professor Jacob Simon George holds a

Doctorate in Philosophy, Doctorate in Ministry, Masters of Arts in Theology and a Bachelors of Arts in Theology. Professor Jacob Simon got employed in Chennai Port Trust where he worked for approximately 10 years. Upon his resignation, he started working full time in Christian ministry where he has served the poor and disadvantaged people with dedication for over 20 years.

As a visionary, Professor Jacob Simon George has created the Good News International University which trains and equips pastors, leaders and believers with knowledge on how to build the Kingdom of God. Good News International University offers degrees and programs in regular stream as well as through distance education. Every year, The Good News International University confers doctoral degrees to eminent persons who serve as leaders and role models to the society. Under Professor Jocob Simon's leadership, the university continues to excel in the theological realm by raising leaders and apostles.

The Good News International University is head quartered in Chennai and has extension centres in Delhi, Mumbai, Uttarakhand and Lucknow in India. Soon, branches will be opened in Sri lanka, Germany and in the Indian provinces of Andhra Pradesh, Lucknow, and Karnataka. For more information, visit www.goodnewsuniversity.org

Professor Jacob Simon has held various positions internationally including:

- President – Good News for Nations Ministries
- Ambassador to Israel - International Human Rights Peace Commission
- National Vice President - iChange Nations
- Advisor for Theological Studies - The Synod of the Pentecostal Churches
- International Director- The Synod of the Pentecostal Churches
- South India Co-Ordinator - International Human Rights Peace Commission
- General Secretary - Leadership Alliance
- Joint Secretary- National Churches of India
- National Co-Ordinator - People's Party of India (Secular).

Professor Jacob Simon has received various awards such as the Ambedkar Award for Social Work, Justice and Peace Award, Presidential Award of Honour and Leadership Excellence Award. As Professor Simon Jacob has consistently engaged in positive action which is transforming his community, we at Greatness University are pleased to recognise him as worthy the title *Icon of Greatness.*

Dr Alwin Roland Timothy, India

Global Peace Ambassador, Humanitarian, Pastor, Leader, Entrepreneur and Philanthropist

Dr Alwin Roland Timothy has been recognised as the Global Peace Ambassador, Humanitarian, Pastor, Leader, Entrepreneur and Philanthropist for his commitment to serving the poor in India. He is the Founder of Global Churches Alliance (GCA), Global Representative of iChange Nations (ICN-USA), Co-Founder of International Human Rights Peace Commission (IHRPC- FL,USA), Asia Representative of US Women Christian Chamber of Commerce, National Director for Government Affairs of the Synod of Pentecostal Churches of India & South Asia, and the Founder and President of World Jesus Mission International.

Bases on his Motto of "Preaching the Healing Word to an Ailing World", Dr Alwin Roland Timothy is fully involved in sharing the message of peace and serving the poor and needy through humanitarian aid, prayer conferences for world peace, seminars, and summits aimed at bringing cultural harmony and peace in the world. He has attended various conferences including the 22nd United nations Human Rights Council in 2013 and the "19th Universal Periodic Review'"(UPR) in 2015 that were held in Geneva, Switzerland.

For four consecutive years since 2014, Dr Alwin Roland Timothy has hosted the World Peace Prayer Conferences and honoured various dignitaries and delegates from all over the world with prestigious awards on behalf of CulturAmbiente, Italy. On 26th January 2016, he was invited as the guest of Honour to hoist the flag during the India Republic Day and afterwards attended the Inter-religious meeting with leaders where they discussed issues related to unity and peace.

In 2016, Dr Alwin Roland Timothy was honoured with the Distinguished Leadership & Community Leadership Award through the International Institute of Leadership & Mentorship, Minnesota, USA (ILM) for his remarkable service to the community and commitment for helping people globally. As Dr Alwin Roland Timothy has served humanity and is a living example of selfless service, we at Greatness University recognise him as worthy of the title *Icon of Greatness.*

Mrs Serena Brown Travis, USA

Daughter of the Legendary Les Brown, Inspirational Speaker, Author and Manager for Les Brown Enterprises

www.serenabrowntravis.com

Serena Brown Travis is an Ohio native and daughter of the legendary motivational speaker Les Brown. Since her and her family's life's work has been full of positivity, motivation, and inspiration, having small goals was not an option. Whilst 'shooting for the moon to land among the stars', Serena earned her Bachelor of Arts degree from Hampton University and got her Master of Arts degree in Marketing and Communication from Franklin University.

She uses her writing to reach young people with her message of positivity. One of her series is titled *The Perfect Penny* which helps children build up their self-esteem in spite of the grim circumstances and ultimately changes their otherwise doomed perspectives into a positive mindset. In *The Perfect Penny*, the daughter of the renowned motivational speaker Les Brown, strategically intertwines disappointment and defeat with messages of encouragement and inspiration.

Outside of viewing the glass half full and acting as the Business Manager for Les Brown Enterprises, Serena enjoys spending time as a volunteer for various non-profit organizations. For more information, visit www.serenabrowntravis.com

We at have reviewed her accomplishments and it is evident that she has stepped into her greatness and positively changed the world. We therefore consider it an honour to bestow upon her the prestigious World Greatness Award. As Serena Brown Travis has served humanity and is a living example of selfless service, we recognise her as worthy of the title *Icon of Greatness.*

Professor Ruben West, USA

Founder of Black Belt Speakers, President of Speaking to Nations, Creator of the International Peaceful Communication Day, and Vision Breakthrough Expert

www.rubenwest.com

Professor Ruben West is truly a one-of-a-kind in the speaking industry. What sets him apart is not just his unique abilities to motivate, transform and inspire on the stage, but rather the vast and varied experiences and successes he achieved prior to taking the stage.

Born in Topeka, Kansas, Professor Ruben West has always had a focus on mastering whatever he set his mind to. 4 years out of high school, at the age of 22, he was promoted to the rank of E-6 Staff Sergeant in the US Army and was awarded for his exemplary efforts in Operation Desert Shield/Storm.

Professor Ruben West and 3 other colleagues helped to start the surgical assistant profession in his home state of Kansas. He co-founded 2 martial arts schools and was inducted into the U. S. Martial Arts Hall of Fame. Together with trusted associates, Dr. West started several businesses, developed patented products all while inspiring others to dream on a larger scale.

Professor Ruben West's convicting messages and lead by example attitude allows him to easily motivate individuals as well as companies to not only aim for the next level but achieve it as well. He is the author and co-author of 10+ books and he continues to be a sought after voice for transformation. He received his PhD and Masters in Positive Neuro Psychology from The American Graduate University of Positive Psychology. He received his Bachelor of Science in Criminal Justice from Washburn University. For more information, visit www.rubenwest.com

Professor Ruben West is the Founder of Black Belt Speakers, Speaking to Nations and he is the Creator of the *International Peaceful Communication Day* that is celebrated around the world every year. In alignment with his book, *A New Communication Paradigm*, Professor Ruben West is asking all of us to participate yearly on 7th October in peaceful communications.

In 2016, Professor Ruben West received the President's Lifetime Achievement Award from President Barack Obama. In 2018 Professor West received the Girma Wolde Giorgis (Former President of Ethiopia) Presidential Award for being a Human Conservationist. In 2019 he received the Sydney Allicock (Vice President of Guyana) Global Humanitarian Award and was recognized as the United States Civility Icon of the Year by iChange Nations™ at the World Civility Day celebration in Gary, Indiana.

As Professor Ruben West has served humanity and is a living example of selfless service, we recognise him as worthy of the title *Icon of Greatness*.

Leading Light of Greatness

The Leading Light of Greatness is offered to those who have been a leading light that has brightly shone and has attracted followers from various parts of the world.

Dr Lul Abdiwahid, Kenya

Founder and CEO of Pure Pearl Foundation, World Civility Ambassador, Among the top 100 most influential Kenyan Muslims, and the World Civility Icon Woman of the Year, Africa 2019

Dr. Lul Abdiwahid is the founder and CEO of Pure Pearl Foundation. Pure Pearl was founded in 2016 and has its main office in Mombasa, Kenya. Its main objective is to transform the lives of vulnerable women, youth and children in Africa through Relief and sustainable economic development projects. Dr. Lul Abdiwahid's inspiration to establish a charitable organisation was triggered by the conflict that exists between the cultural beliefs and the prosperity of women and youths in the local communities. She witnessed first-hand the effects of harmful practices on victims of female genital mutilation, gender based violence, child marriages, and the general women's struggle for basic human rights. This experience drove her to think of effective ways to solve this problem.

After obtaining a law degree from the UK, Dr. Lul Abdiwahid joined the Kenya School of Law, got admitted to the Bar, and set up a law firm called Abdiwahid and Associates. Through her practice, she has handled over 100 pro bono cases on gender inequality, discrimination and gender based violence.

Dr. Lul Abdiwahid is also the founder of Salu Solutions Ltd: one of the most competitive professional cleaning and waste management companies in Kenya. This company specialises in professional cleaning services for industrial, commercial and domestic needs having served over 150 prestigious businesses. Since its inception, the company has created employment for over 110 youths and women who traditionally couldn't be employed due to their lack of the requisite experience and qualifications.

Dr. Lul Abdiwahid is passionate about women and youth empowerment. She hopes that time will come when equal opportunities will be available to everyone no matter their gender. Economic and social justice for every woman, youth and child in Africa continues to be her dream. Through her foundation, Dr. Abdiwahid's vision to have an educated and skillful population in the near future is being fulfilled gradually. She believes that a peaceful living community will be attained by empowering the masses and that is her major focus.

Furthermore, Dr. Abdiwahid's high level interaction with government officials, special envoys and global leaders has led Pure Pearl Foundation to become a force to recon with in the East African Region. This was evident in the 2019 Global Women Conference (GWC) hosted by the foundation. The 2019 GWC was the first of its own kind in the region where renowned inspirational speakers from all over the world graced the event. The keynote speaker was the Secretary General of UNCTAD – United Nation Conference of Trade and Development - Dr. Mukhisa Kituyi. Other speakers included: Jacqueline Mims, a Former Aerospace Technologist at NASA; Professor Reuben West, an expert in motivational speaking and corporate training; H.E Hassan Joho, the Governor of Mombasa; and Di Downie, a solution specialist among others.

Due to her work and studies, Dr Lul Abdiwahid has been honoured with a Doctorate in Humanities from United Graduate College and Seminary International, USA; a Masters in International Law (LLM) from the University of

Warwick, England; and LLB from University of Kent, Canterbury. She has been awarded the World Civility Ambassador, and Ambassador for Peace from the Universal Federation of Peace. She has also been named among the top 100 most influential Kenyan Muslim, and most recently she was named the World Civility Icon Woman of the Year, Africa 2019. Additionally, Dr. Lul Abdiwahid is member of the Law society of Kenya (LSK), Mombasa Law Society (MLS), Federation of Women Lawyers in Kenya (FIDA), Chartered Institute of Arbitrators (CIARB Kenya), iChange Nations and also a member of the Standards Tribunal. She is an entrepreneur, an advocate of the High Court of Kenya and a philanthropist who enjoys reading motivational books and traveling.

Based on her work and real-time achievements, it is evident that Dr. Lul Abdiwahid has aligned herself to her greatness and created new paths. We at Greatness University consider it an honour to bestow upon her the prestigious World Greatness Award. As she has been a leading light that is shining brightly and attracting followers from various parts of the world, we recognise her as a Leading Light of Greatness.

Dr Frank Kanu Kanu, Sweden

Founder and President of The Organization for Poverty Alleviation Development Global (OPAD)

Dr Frank Kanu Kanu is an ardent campaigner against the excessive use of drugs and alcohol among young people, discrimination, and the inequality of opportunities in Sweden. Dr Kanu Kanu has also campaigned for peace and solidarity to end hunger, poverty, and worked towards the promotion of democracy and human rights in the second and third world countries. He is passionate about eradicating youth gang violence, child sexual exploitation, and providing free learning centre for refugees. In this endeavor, he has worked with NGOs and civil societies at local, national and international levels.

Dr Frank Kanu Kanu is Founder and President of *The Organization for Poverty Alleviation Development Global (OPAD)* that reconnects the poor and marginalized communities who have global aspirations of making the world a better place for all. OPAD works with the youth, women and children as the pivot for change that does not only require aid but also capacity and skills for turning the Sustainable Development Goals' (SDGs) dreams into reality. Committed to its vision of "An Equitable Society free from Human Suffering" whether in developed, developing or underdeveloped countries; OPAD has a footprint in over 50 countries. OPAD is one of the implementers of Beneficiaries Led Aid [BLA] in Poverty Alleviation Programmes, Climate change Mitigation, relief, conflict resolution and Human Health in our strategic countries of operations.

Dr Frank Kanu Kanu was born in Sierra Leone in West Africa. Raised in a middle-class family, he started his education journey at the Methodist Boys High School.

He was later accepted at the University of Aden in the UK where he studied for a Bachelor of Arts in Social Studies. Dr Kanu Kanu passion for learning has led him to also study for a Bachelor of Arts degree in Business Management (Honors) at the University of Bologna, Italy; and an MBA Sociology at the University of Aden, United Kingdom. He has been honoured by the United Graduate College and Seminary international with a Doctorate in Leadership and Governance. These qualification and awards have been instrumental in him being a voice for the poor and the disadvantaged in our societies and being a messenger who exposes these issues to the general public, civil society, governments, UN bodies and other international actors. His motto is the words of the Great Nelson Mandela who said, "Education is the great engine of personal development. It is through education that the daughter of a peasant can become a doctor, that the son of a mineworker can become the head of the mine that a child of farm workers can become the president of a great nation. It is what we make out of what we have, not what we are given, that separates one person from another."

Dr Frank Kanu Kanu has occupied various leadership positions including: being OPAD UN Permanent Representative; Vice President and Board Director of the Youth International Initiative , Sweden; and Vice President and Board Director International the Organization for Democracy and Human Rights. As Dr Frank Kanu Kanu he has been a leading light that is shining and attracting followers from various parts of the world, we recognise him as a *Leading Light of Greatness.*

Dr Tshibangu Mukumbay, DRC

Founder of 'Union du Peuple d' Avenir (UPA)'/ United People with One Destiny, A Dynamic Coach, and Progressive Advocator of fairness, Equality and the Eradication of Human Suffering

Ambassador Tshibangu Mukumbay, PhD was born in 1966 in Kinshasa, DRC. He has sojourned in many countries such as Ivory Coast, Switzerland and now resides both in the United Kingdom and the DRC. He is an independent business consultant and brings investors and business opportunities to Africa. He also helps in creating teams of governmental officials who bring to life dormant projects in Africa by creating necessary contact with investors. For example, he has organised international investors to visit project locations in the Congo DR (South Kivu, Kinshasa, Kasai-Oriental, Maniema, Bas-Congo and Mpweto in Katanga).

Dr Mukumbay is a lead negotiator with private investors to tackle projects in mining, road construction, environmental impact assessment and instigating project to effect the most convicting burden – "Building and Promoting the Land and the people of Africa". His expertise involves trading in high temperature ores (copper, cobalt, coltan, cassiterite, etc), gold and diamond. He traded in heavy industrial equipments and organizing shipping and delivery to the Democratic Republic of Congo, Zambia, Tanzania, Sierra Leone and Ghana.

Dr Mukumbay is a visionary with insight, a dynamic coach and mentor, a progressive advocator of fairness, equality and eradication of human suffering. He enjoys reading and political debates. He is good communicator with a natural skill for diplomacy, negotiating in business and conflict resolution. He loves football and karate. He likes to take risks, challenges, traveling and reaching the forgotten ones such as the Pygmies in DR Congo. He led a team of artisanal miners in

Mpweto/Katanga's province digging copper and another team of artisanal miners in Bakua Tshimuna/Kasai-Oriental's province digging Diamond.

At the heart of all his activities is the desire to serve others. That makes him a man on a mission. This is exemplified in his commitment to the *Union du Peuple d' Avenir (UPA)* or United People with One Destiny which was established with a commitment to keeping the Democratic Republic of Congo's sovereignty, territorial integrity and prosperity by uniting all Congolese people in order to provide the opportunity for sustainable development. Since the inception of the UPA, Dr Mukumbay and his executive team have been very active in preparation for the leadership by traveling to different countries visiting companies, industries, factories, manufacturers and meeting political leaders, businessmen, journalists, religious leaders, human rights activists, nation builders and others to acquire experience in various governmental sectors so that they can implement the UPA's vision of "Build and Promote the Land".

Two traits that personifies Dr Tshibangu Mukumbay; a charismatic leader and a man of unwavering character. His motto is "The one God has chosen does not fight for a position, instead he prepares himself; because God will always position him in due time". As he has been a leading light that is shining brightly and attracting followers from various parts of the world, we recognise Dr Tshibangu Mukumbay as a *Leading Light of Greatness.*

Dr Justina Mutale, UK

African Woman of the Year, International Speaker, Philanthropist, Global Influencer, and Founder of the Justina Mutale Foundation

www.justinamutale.com

Her Excellence Dr Justina Mutale has been globally acclaimed as one of the most influential and inspirational women of African origin. In 2012, she was awarded the prestigious title of *'African Woman of the Year'*. She is named in the 100 Most Reputable People on Earth and 100 Most Reputable Africans in the World. Dr Mutale is also listed in the Powerlist of the 100 Most Influential African Women; 100 Most Influential Black People in the United Kingdom; and the BLACK 100+ Hall of Fame, an Exhibition and Legacy of the top 100 Black Achievers in modern Britain.

Dr Mutale serves on the Board of the World Leaders Forum. She is also Global Envoy for Gender Equality and Spokesperson of the International Women's Think Tank. In addition, Dr Mutale is a Mentor and Consultant to the Young Africa Leaders Forum. A globally acclaimed and most sought-after International Keynote Speaker, Dr Mutale is a regular Keynote Speaker at various Economic Forums around the world and other high-level conferences and meetings that address Political, Economic, Social, Gender and African Issues. She is a delegate and Speaker at the United Nations Commission on the Status of Women, as well as the African Union High-Level Panel on Gender Equality and the Commonwealth Women's Forum. Dr Mutale is a Distinguished Member of the Royal Biographical Institute, in addition to being a Distinguished Member of Global Order of Dignitaries an honour bestowed upon her in the Global Officials of Dignity (G.O.D.) Awards at a ceremony held at the United Nations Headquarters in New York.

Dr. Mutale is the Founder and President of the *Justina Mutale Foundation*. She is also the Founder of *POSITIVE RUNWAY: Global Catwalk to Stop the Spread of HIV/AIDS*. Through her own Foundation, Dr Mutale advocates for gender equality and the empowerment of women and girls, including the economic empowerment of women by providing entrepreneurship and leadership training and mentorship. She also advocates for the retention and completion of tertiary education for young women and girls, as well as boys from rural and disadvantaged families in Africa by providing them with university scholarships to access higher education around the world. Dr Mutale has been acclaimed as a game changer and is featured among African women who are changing the game, changing the rules and changing the future. She has been praised as one of the 21st century new leaders and influencers of our time, who are challenging what we have known for ages, challenging the stereotypes, challenging the norms and creating their own reality, which resonates with the needs of people around them, leaders who lead by maximising resources around them to create powerful ripple effects that are changing lives around the world, using the power of her gifting, vision and creativity. She has been globally recognised as a public personality who has the ability to use her status to potentially influence new thinking, to inspire the future, motivate the young generation, and make the world a better place.

A recipient of numerous other Awards, Honours and Accolades across the globe, Dr Mutale has been honoured with seven different Honorary Doctorates. She is listed on numerous Halls of Fame, WHO's WHO Lists, Influential Lists and Power Lists around the world. She serves as President, Patron, Ambassador, Chairperson, Trustee, Consultant, and Mentor to various organisation in the UK and across the globe. Dr Mutale has been honoured for her outstanding and phenomenal leadership qualities as a Stateswoman; Global Woman Leader of the Year, and Iconic Woman Leader of the Decade. www.justinamutale.com

Based on her work and real-time achievements, it is evident that Her Excellence Dr. Justina Mutale has aligned herself to her greatness and created new paths. We at Greatness University consider it an honour to bestow upon her the prestigious World Greatness Award. As she has been a leading light that is shining brightly and attracting followers from various parts of the world, we recognise her as a *Leading Light of Greatness.*

Dr Oluwafemi T Ogunjinmi, USA

Global Relationship New Rule Expert, Award Winning Motivational Speaker, Talk Show host and Creator of the National Relationship Equity Day

Dr. Femi Ogunjinmi, also known as Gfem is a sought after Global relationship new rule expert, certified life coach, award winning motivational speaker, teacher of the word, and talk show host who has been improving the lives of singles and couples for over ten years. He has authored two edition books titled, "Revelations of Relationship: What you don't know about finding true love and sustaining relationship." The second edition of the book has been placed at local library including Barnes & Noble store in Harford County, Maryland, USA.

Dr. Femi is a go-to expert to media outlets like USA TODAY MAGAZINE, FOX NEWS, and STYLECASTER. He has spoken on big media platforms including The Word Network, RADIO ONE, SIRIUS XM, SPLASH FM, and TEDx. His speech on TEDx received over 2million views within nine months of its release and growing by 100,000 views every month.

Apart from keynoting and speaking at conferences across the United State and overseas, Dr. Femi also conducts his own relationship programs. His signature conference, "Revelations of Relationship Seminar" occurs every year in United State and has been conducted internationally in Nigeria. Dr. Femi's list of workshops includes "Becoming The Man She Wants" & "Becoming The Person Your Partner Wants".

Dr. Femi is the founder of National Relationship Equity Day, an organization that has created a national awareness day celebrated June 24th of every year. National

Relationship Equity Day is dedicated to eradicating gender inequity in relationship and promoting the use of gifts, values, skill sets, and interests as a way of defining roles in relationship other than gender.

As a scholar, Dr. Femi earned his Bachelor of Science in Biology from Morgan State University, graduated with Master in Business Administration from Benedictine University, possesses a Cybersecurity Certification, and was conferred an Honorary Doctorate of Humanities by United Graduate College and Seminary.

Based on his work and real-time achievements, it is evident that Dr Oluwafemi T Ogunjinmi has aligned himself to his greatness. We at Greatness University consider it an honour to bestow upon him the prestigious World Greatness Award. As he has been a leading light that is shining brightly and attracting followers from various parts of the world, we recognise him as a *Leading Light of Greatness.*

Dr Tony Elkhier Jaja, South Sudan

Founder of Union of Churches for Peace initiatives in Sudan (UCPIS)

Dr. Tony E. Jaja is the founder of the Union of Churches for Peace initiatives in Sudan (UCPIS): a movement focused not only on carrying out the gospel of Jesus Christ, but also on bring peace and reconciliation to the Sudanese people who have not experienced peace since independence and also be a model to other African countries who experience the same conflicts. He is fluent in English, Arabic, Swahili and Dinka.

As a statesman, Dr. Tony E. Jaja has had various roles including being:

- *World Civility Ambassador*
- *Global Adviser for I Change Nations*
- *Member of pan African fusion and Peace Expert*
- *Advisor for the United Graduate College and Seminary International*
- *Member of international Christian Chamber of Commerce*
- *Special Representative for the International Human Rights Peace Commission in Horn, East and North Africa.*

Dr Tony Jaja has had many offices and carries out diverse functions including:

- *Coordinator at United Nations Global Compact Business for Peace Initiative South Local Network 2014-2017*
- *Chief Ambassador for Israel South Sudan Chapter 2012-2015*
- *Secretary of foreign affairs for South Sudan Business Union 2012 – 2017*
- *Board member of South Supreme Airline's South Sudan 2013 - 2016*

- Member of Black Chamber of Commerce USA 2011-2017
- Top Adviser to the Ambassador at large for the Republic of Burundi Dr. Clyde Rivers on the Issues of Burundi in Australia and the South Pacific 2011- 2010
- Member of Full Gospel Businesswoman Fellowship International Australia Chapter 2009 - 2012
- Member of International Centre for Religious and Diplomatic USA 2000-2002
- CEO and Chairman of Board of Directors of JAJA AIR and Golden Dove International LTD
- Founder of Conquer the World Faith Ministers International

Dr. Tony Jaja is the recipient of World Civility award and an honorary doctorate from the United Graduate College and Seminary International.

Based on his work and real-time achievements, it is evident that Dr. Tony Jaja has aligned himself to his greatness and created new paths. We at Greatness University consider it an honour to bestow upon him the prestigious World Greatness Award. As he has been a leading light that is shining brightly and attracting followers from various parts of the world, we recognise him as a *Leading Light of Greatness.*

Professor Chris O. Imafodin, UK

World Renowned Adviser to Presidents, Governments, Monarchs and Leaders

www.imafidons.com

Professor Chris Imafidon is a “world renowned adviser to Monarchs, Governments, Presidents and Corporate leaders” according to ABC/CBS News. International news agencies describe him as "a legend” after his students broke multiple world records". CNN journalists refer to him as an "intellectual icon". He is a New York Times quoted authority. The BBC and Sky News refer to him as the patriarch of the "world's smartest family". He is a multi-award winning pioneer and currently chairs the board of directors of the Excellence in Education programme – world-wide. (www.ExcellenceinEducation.org.uk)

Professor Imafidon – is regarded as one of the “world’s foremost scholars on leveraging informatics for learning and exceptional achievement (genius)” according to the BBC, CNN and USA-Today journalists. He quote has been published by TIME magazine. His keynote speeches inspires and motivates audience to quadruple their productivity and reveals their hidden geniuses and leadership talents. In the days following the publication of President Barack Obama’s Op-ed in the British *Telegraph* newspaper, Professor Chris Imafidon was invited to write an Op-ed featured article for the *Sunday Times*. He has subsequently been invited to write another piece for the UK’s *Financial Times*. "Leading Harvard and Cambridge University professors have recognised him as "the patriarch of modern education and informatics” Professor Chris Imafidon served on the Board of Governors, Woodford' one of the nation's most successful schools and runs special programmes to help disadvantages students and inner-city children to access top institutions and prestigious scholarships in academics, sports, music, the arts and languages [www.Imafidons.com]. In recognition of Professor Imafidon's collaboration in STEM teaching and research, he was one of the few scholars at Westminster Abbey for the final internment of Sir Stephen Hawking.

Prof. Chris Imafidon's highly acclaimed results/publications have served as benchmarks for policy development. He was nicknamed by Yahoo News (Finance) as "the author of the most anticipated bestsellers" on International relations of UK/EU. His book on the Monarchy received a special award at the BAFTA recently. He has lectured on Human Capital Development under the auspices of the UNDP and other UN agencies. He has been a guest/visiting professor to leading American Universities namely Harvard, Cornell, Columbia, SUNY, Georgetown, Miami, and Louisiana State University and he collaborates with researchers at Yale University.

Professor Chris Imafidon has featured in several real-time presentations in over 4,500 major media outlets. He has been invited on three different occasions on the Oprah Winfrey TV Show (USA). His ubiquitous intellectual contributions have attracted rave comments from several global media outlets. He was described by the BBC and Sky News as the patriarch of the "world's most mathematical family". Prof. Chris Imafidon is a man who walks the talk. He mentors several geniuses across the world and has demonstrated this within his family, thus the appellation: Patriarch of "Britain's brainiest" or "smartest family". The academic, musical and sporting achievements of his children, and mentees are eloquent testimonies to this epithet. They are truly chips off the old block. His daughter, Dr Anne-Marie Imafidon, MBE who speaks six languages became the youngest person to pass the UK A-level computing examination at only 11 in 2003. At 13, she won a national to attend John Hopkins University in Baltimore, USA and later got her Master's degree with specialty in Mathematical computation, at the age of 19, from Oxford University. Dr Anne-Marie Imafidon recently became the youngest Fortune 100 manager and also the youngest scientist ever honored by Queen Elizabeth of the UK. She is now listed in BBC's top 100 most influential woman. She now champions the initiative to empower more girls to study Science, Technology, Engineering and Mathematics (STEM).

Another daughter, Christina Imafidon, was the youngest student ever to study at undergraduate degree level at the tender age of 11 at any British university; and became a choral scholar at the University of Oxford (Hertford). Samantha Imafidon, his third child, passed two high school-level Mathematics and Statistics examinations at age 6, and mentored her younger twin siblings. She studied computer science degree while she was a choral scholar at Baliol College, Oxford and have received many invitations from HM Queen Elizabeth II. Twins, Peter and Paula Imafidon broke three world records at the age of 7 and was nicknamed "Wonder Twins" by leading media. They later passed the University of Cambridge Foundations of Mathematics at a mere age of 8, thereby setting another new world record. Till date, they are the youngest children in British history to attend high school. Peter Imafidon is rated by FIFA as the top 100 footballers for his age, while holding three different world records in Mathematics. While Paula was invited as a county champion in rugby and also represented team Great Britain in Hockey. Professor Imafidon and his family were invited to front row seats as guests at a special 90th birthday service held in Windsor Castle for Her Majesty, Queen Elizabeth II, in April 2016. Also, Professor Imafidon has had the privilege of being one of the leaders who have hosted His Eminence, Martin Schulz, the President of the European parliament. The Imafidons have been featured by Forbes Magazine (USA), Washington Post, New York Times; SkyTV, Financial Times.

In a correspondence with American's best-selling newspaper, USA Today, Harvard educated Professor Maxwell described Professor Imafidon as "the finest educationist ever on planet earth, adding that he has invented an innovative learning methodology (#GeniusFormula) for easily bringing out the genius in any child – irrespective Of gender, class or background".

World revered, Professor William Maxwell (EdD Harvard) characterised Professor Chris Imafidon as "an outstanding, remarkable, selfless, tireless, man who weekly carries out unpaid work and unseen mentoring of inner-city children over two decades. Adding that Prof Imafidon is making a great change in the lives of young people within disadvantaged, communities, schools, colleges. Professor Imafidon through his keynote speaking, and practical programmes guides and inspires youths of all backgrounds and genders across the nation to attend top universities and gain top jobs. According to the popular press, Prof Imafidon's unrecognised phenomenally inspirational work has had a great impact on the next generation which he started in Waltham Forest in 1998. It now has students from every borough in the UK, abroad.

It is common knowledge that Professor Chris Imafidon devised and implemented a new formula (#GeniusFormula) to raise leaders from inner-city youths and children of disadvantaged backgrounds to top university and mentors them to become leaders in their industry.

The huge contributions of Prof Chris Imafidon who raised the highest number of inner-city child prodigies and whose dedication, personal sacrifice and new formula of teaching difficult subject or concepts via gamification has been successfully implemented by his protégés at the world's top universities and leading industries. His principles and methods are now being used by leaders, governments and institutions in Europe, Asia, America and Africa. Prof Imafidon co-founded Excellence In Education programme when he discovered that the gifts and talents of his children's classmates were undetected or under-developed, and leadership skills were stifled in most youths.

Professor Imafidon leads the EIE programme which runs free seminars and workshops, webinar, and mentoring schemes for parents, teachers, schools and institutions in inner cities across the world. He holds conferences for leading institutions on raising achievements and human capital developments. Many government, or charity or privately-run organisations have implemented new techniques of EIE to achieve record breaking results.

Professor Chris Imafidon also contributes to entrepreneurship teaching and training in the UK, USA, China and internationally. He currently runs special programs on accelerated learning with Professor William Maxwell (EdD Harvard) and have received invitations for a state-visit from the government of Montana (USA).

Professor Imafidon has appeared on BBC TV News and *SkyTV* news to discuss topical issues. He has been on National BBC and spoke on education and received huge cry from the public to be Secretary of State for Education. Prof Imafidon rejected all invitations to serve in the official national inquiry into London's Grenfell tower fire – Britain's worst an inner-city housing tragedy.

Professor Imafidon and his students have been invited to appear on the *Ellen DeGeneres/HBO Max* TV Show (USA). He has mentored students who became record breakers in all major exams. His students have been featured in all UK & European major media (Including *BBC, ITV, Times, Guardian, Telegraph, The Mail, Standard, Mirror, Sun, & Oxford Mail*). His students and mentees have also been published by US *TIME* magazine, *Financial Times, Forbes Magazine* and have been invited to address NATO, and IEEE conferences. He acts as a training consultant to local and national government in Technology, Leadership and Education amongst others. He has inspired a lot of his students who have become captains of top industries, or leaders in academia all over the world.

In July 2014, Professor Chris Imafidon was named as one of the top 100 people who have made the greatest contribution in the last 100 years in the UK. He is a former head of the Management of Technology Unit at Queen Mary College, University of London. He has mentored various Masters/PhD degree studies including various aspects of computer security health/medicine, entrepreneurship and informatics. And he continues to mentor, supervise or act as Examiner for various PhD, and post-graduates students Russell group universities.

During Professor Imafidon's tenure of office as a board member, Woodford won a grant of two million pounds (£2,000,000.00) - the highest grant ever in its entire history. During the early stages of the web commercial usage, Professor Imafidon used internet based technologies to start an on-line publication which he pioneered as European Editor and generated about one million pounds (£1,000,000.00) in the first year. Earlier, building on the subject of his Masters thesis, Dr Imafidon attracted about one million pounds (£1,000,000.00) in equipment grant for a computerised study of the human eye.

In 1992 he was an invited guest to *'Equinox'* - a Canadian Radio programme which features eminent scholars and world renowned researchers to discuss the findings of his pioneering study. He has lectured in all the continents of the world from Africa, to Asia, to America and Europe. Professor Chris continues to attract numerous invitations from prestigious institutions in Europe, USA, Asia and Africa to speak at major conferences, seminars and universities. He has written or provided inspiration for hundreds of journal papers and books. He is the most cited author in aspects of scientific research. Prof Chris Imafidon is mentoring/educating disadvantaged young adults, youths and inner-city children across the nations to attend top universities and gain top jobs. This is inspired by the Mandelian dictum of "Education being the most powerful weapon that can change the world"

Based on his work and real-time achievements, it is evident that Prof Chris Imafodin has aligned himself to his greatness. We at Greatness University consider it an honour to bestow upon him the prestigious World Greatness Award. As he has been a leading light that is shining brightly and attracting followers from various parts of the world, we recognise him as a *Leading Light of Greatness.*

Mr Chris Perry, UK

Founder of Strategy for One Consultancy, Educator, and Creator of the "Uncluttered Bible": the first Interactive Bible on iBooks

Chris Perry has a unique story. There is no better way to tell it than in his words:

I came across Ambassador Dr Clyde Rivers, who nominated me for this award, through Dr Ivy Bonk from Delaware (USA) a few years ago but met him in person in the early part of 2019 in London. He opened my eyes to the term 'Unlimited' and his own testimony reveals the impact of the power of belief to affect many nations and leaders who he has visited and consulted with.

While at a University in Wales early in my career a lecturer introduced to my fellow students and me a fantastic course on 'Strategy' and some great insights by Prof Michael E Porter (Harvard) from the USA that 'innovation is the key to personal, town, city or national success'. This caused a spark in me that has never gone out! Pictures in my heart and mind continued to form and grow. This has directly contributed to my unique approach to make learning an enjoyable and fun experience. So I entered both the IT Training and Career consultancy industries, worldwide. My clients have gained employment (at least £45m) to financially support their families.

Grateful to God for saving my mother and I from certain death, pregnant with me, where my father was a civil engineer on contract at a leading industrial steel city in India during early 50s. She had boarded the Comet plane in Calcutta in 1953, so I could be born in the UK. She was ill and the captain took the decision to remove us off the flight. He, his staff and all passengers lost their lives! Now 66 years old I am still consulting and writing as well as having ideas for books, podcasts and inventions. But I do want to say a big thank you to all the many wonderful people I have had the honour over the years to meet, who inspired me and have helped me to become the success, I am today.

In 2020 I will launch my new book called the ARC Paradigm, a relationship model to enable people to see the path of their key development and play a unique part in this world, with their gifts and talents. Each generation builds on previous innovations and learning, yet the potential now is global in its reach through access to modern technology! I remember getting so excited to use a golf ball electric typewriter, never thinking I would use voice recognition software to speak my words directly via my mobile!!

My key achievements over the last 30 years have been:

- Freelance consultant to one of the top career companies in Europe. I later became the leading consultant by results of their 70 consultants worldwide, with a 96% success record to help people find employment at various levels.
- My own business - Strategy for One Consultancy has for a number of years continued being successful to the current time, still inspiring through personal mentoring, CV and Resume writing, as well as Course Development.
- Many satisfied clients ranged across the world from the USA to Europe, Africa, Caribbean and many more. The industries and professions were very varied from Oil and Gas to Education and Hospitality, also Tourism, Banking, Insurance, Law, the BBC and many more. I have interviewed and advised a wide number of

people in management roles to people facing redundancy and sense of hopelessness, to young people excited at the start of their careers. We all have made a contribution to the world of work.

- Chosen within a small team (1998 to early 2000) to train in IT all Her Majesty's Ambassadors and entire staff across the globe.
- CEO of the UK Institute of IT Training awarded me Membership status, one short of a Fellow for my contribution to the UK and global IT training to improve 1,000s of people to grow in confidence and expertise to meet the challenges of new software and its use.
- Trained and wrote innovative materials for companies such as Hewlett Packard, British Airways, Rolls Royce and Sir Terry Mathews, CEO of multimillion company (Newbridge Networks) and many others to use Microsoft Office and create bespoke courses.
- Created the first interactive Bible on the Apple iBooks platform in 2012, called the Uncluttered Bible. This took 9 months full time to reformat the entire Bible without numbers and headings to give a new way of reading the Scriptures.
- Diploma in Biblical Studies (2 years) at the famous Bible College of Wales.
- Post Graduate Certificate in Education ((FE), Cardiff University.
- BA (Hons) in Business Studies, University of Glamorgan.

Based on his work and real-time achievements, it is evident that Mr Chris Perry has aligned himself to his greatness. We at Greatness University consider it an honour to bestow upon him the *Leading Light of Greatness* award.

Creators of Greatness

Creators of Greatness Award is given to people who have consistently engaged in positive action and transformed their communities.

Miss Loubna Ammer, UAE

Middle East Business Consultant

Loubna Ammer is a Middle East Business Consultant. She is an expert in identifying business opportunities in the Middle East such as the United Arab Emirates and creating bespoke business partnerships with companies in Europe. She is also set out to find and create meaningful businesses relationships with entrepreneurs and businesses in Asia, Africa, and America. Her entrepreneurial mindset allows her to unlock opportunities in various areas of business and her clientele includes: construction businesses, film festivals, international education shows, speakers, leaders, authors, entrepreneurs and governmental authorities.

Born and raised in Syria, Loubna Ammer holds a Bachelor's degree in English Literature from Damascus University and a Master's degree in English/ Arabic Translation and Interpreting from the American University of Sharjah in the United Arab Emirates. Loubna has worked and lived in various countries including the United Arab Emirates, Turkey, and Germany where she is based.

Loubna Ammer has wide experience as an interpreter to government departments and private organisations. For more than 14 years, she has translated from English into Arabic and vice versa in fields related to personal development, education, economy, marketing, and business among others. She also has an extensive experience of editing and proofreading from Arabic to English. As she has consistently acted as a bridge between the East and the West through her translation, interpretation, and consultancy work, we at recognise Miss Loubna Ammer as worthy of the title *Creator of Greatness.*

Dr John Inico Prabhu James Durairaj, India

Ordained Minister, Travelling Evangelist and Founder of Nations Trumpet Ministries

Rev. Dr. JOHN INICO PRABHU is an ordained minister and a travelling evangelist in India. He started his ministry through street preaching, tract distribution, village ministry, tribal ministry, film ministry, hospital visiting, children ministry, and youth ministry while he was 13 years old.

He holds a Master's degree in divinity. He is the founder of *Nations Trumpet Ministries* in the south of India. He has a strong passion of raising the next generation of leaders. With this zeal, he goes on mission trips in India and overseas where he conducts gospel crusades, youth conferences, television programmes, and teaching in power camps. He recently received an Honorary Doctorate in Ministry from *The Good News International University*, Chennai, India.

As he has consistently engaged in positive action and he is actively transforming his community, we at Greatness University recognise Dr John Inico Prabhu as a *Creator of Greatness.*

Dr Raymond Harlall, Canada

World Civility Ambassador, Motivational Speaker, Serial Entrepreneur, Philanthropist, International Consultant, and Book Publisher

www.raymondharlall.com

The World Civility Ambassador Dr. Raymond Harlall PhD (h.c) is a motivational speaker, serial entrepreneur, philanthropist, international consultant, and representative to the United Nations. Dr. Harlall, has joint ventures around the Globe with business partners, his co-authors and fellow Ambassadors. He uses his relationship capital to bridge the gap between governments, NGOs, local leaders and at risk communities.

As an advocate for the United Nation's *17 Sustainable Development Goals* (SDGs) achievement by 2030, Ambassador Harlall travels to developing countries to empower young entrepreneurs in their own communities. His Global initiative is called *iEmpower Entrepreneurs™*. He strongly believes that we can end poverty through Public-Private Partnerships. As such, he is known as *The Global Developer™* of Human Currency™ .

This Canadian based Guyanese has been featured in multiple local and international media outlets for his many achievements as he journeyed from an immigrant labourer to business owner and global influencer in less than 5 years. At 30 years old, Dr Harlall is a husband and father, actively managing several businesses and author of eight books. He is also a multiple times #1 International Bestselling Author on Amazon, he is also the recipient of several awards, including the Global Author's Award 2018 in the United Kingdom, World Civility Award

2019 in the USA, Honorary PhD in Humanities in Uganda, and The Nelson Mandela International Peace Award 2019 in Sri Lanka.

As a book publisher, Dr. Harlall has started his own non-fiction book series endorsed by legends like Dr. Brian Tracy and Mr. Les Brown. Raymond hosts and produces *The Power of Collaboration*; a world-class personal and business development annual event in Toronto. He is the founder of Canada Book Club & Expo. As president of Local Experts Group, he works to promote micro-economics in developed nations. Raymond is now pooling his resources with investors to establish *The Small Business Development Capital™* investment fund in Guyana, to be launched first quarter of 2020, in an effort to actively support sustainable initiatives and new macro-economies in his homeland that are in line with the 17 UN SDGs.

Based on his work and real-time achievements, it is evident that Dr Raymond Harlall has created greatness. We at Greatness University consider it an honour to bestow upon him the prestigious World Greatness Award. As he has consistently engaged in positive action and he is actively transforming his community, we recognise him as worthy of the title *Creator of Greatness.*

www.greatness-university.com

Connect with Raymond Harlall on how to get published in his series

www.raymondharlall.com

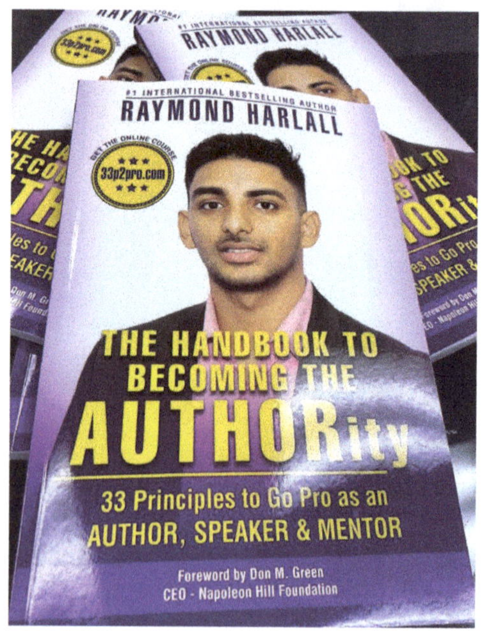

Dr Christine R Kozachuk, USA

World Civility Ambassador, International Speaker, Entrepreneur, and Author

Dr. Christine Kozachuk is a World Civility Ambassador, International Speaker, Entrepreneur, and Author. She owns multiple successful businesses such as RC Mobile Truck Repair Services and Every Girl Wins Institute that helps women rewrite the definition of their lives. She is a Co-Host of The Real Business Women Of Charlotte.

Dr. Kozachuk was the Managing Director of Charlotte's International eWomenNetwork-ing group for over two years. She successfully opened and operated two fitness studios: Pink Ice Ladies Fitness Center and Fit N Free for Life in which she not only ran the studios but instructed and encouraged every client. She has also served on the board of Home4Me for over two years. Home4Me provides our teens and young adults in foster care with guidance, mentoring and encouragement at the time in their lives when they need it most.

Dr. Kozachuk has been recognised with the following awards:

- 2010 Give First Share Always by eWomenNetwork
- 2017 Share my Voice by Black Belt Speakers
- 2017 Leverage Leader by eWomenNetwork
- 2018 Women Add Value by iChange Nations
- 2018 Leadership by iChange Nations
- 2018 Voice of Change by iChange Nations
- 2019 World Civility award by iChange Nations

- 2019 Susan M Gibson Golden Microphone by Black Belt Speakers
- 2019 Vernet A. Joseph Productive Global Agent of Change.

Dr. Kozachuk has written and co-authored several books including:

- How Can I Create the Life I Deserve? (K.N.O.C.K. Formula)
- Live Your Best Life-Walk by Faith
- Letters of Love, Dear Loved One
- The Chronicles of The Chosen-Living Life by Design
- Do It Yourself Podcast-Step by Step Guide for Beginners
- Meditation MP3 called Freeing Yourself from The Chains of The Past.

As Dr Christine Kozachuk has consistently engaged in positive action and she is actively transforming her community, we at Greatness University recognise her as worthy of the title *Creator of Greatness.*

Mr Allan Mandindi, UK

Activist, Writer, and Entrepreneur

Allan Mandindi is an Activist, Writer, Entrepreneur, community worker and former member of the British Armed Forces. He was born in Lilongwe: the capital city of Malawi, from a modest family of seven, four boys and three girls. He migrated to the United Kingdom in 2003 after finishing his secondary school to study Accounting at Emile Woolf College in Manchester.

At an early stage of his studies, he realised that accounting was not for him. Through a friend who was in the British Army who came to visit him, he was persuaded to join the British Army where he served for 5 years. During those years, he was posted to Germany, Cyprus and Afghanistan where in 2011 he was awarded the Afghanistan Service Medal. When he left the army in 2013, he studied political science at Manchester Metropolitan University where he graduated in 2017 with with an Honours Degree in Politics and a Master's Degree in International Relations and Global Communication and 2018.

In 2016, Allan Mandindi became a co-founder of the Maravi Heritage Foundation: an organization that was founded by members of the Malawian Diaspora with the aim of engaging in humanitarian and empowering Malawian Communities abroad and home. Its main focus is promoting Malawian culture and values through engaging with Malawian businesses, conducting research and nurturing transformative ideas that empower the African Diaspora. Maravi Foundation has volunteers around the world who carry out various community based projects. So far, it has a media project in Manchester that identifies

Malawian talent in the diaspora and promotes them. It also have land conservation project 'One Tree One Citizen" and an Albino empowerment project in Malawi. Due to its good work, Maravi Heritage Foundation has received an award of Excellence from Trumpet Media Groups at this year's 21st Annual Gathering of Africa's Best Award which was held at Manchester Hilton.

Allan Mandindi is very involved in community activities and politics. He is a Board member of his local community school as governor. He is the vice Chair of his local Labour Party Branch of Openshaw and Clayton. He is also very active in Malawian politics as Vice Chair of the Malawi Congress Party Diaspora. Allan Mandindi enjoys expressing himself through writing his thoughts in various media platforms and has been a co-author of *Archbishop Doye T Agama Changed Our Lives*: an anthology that documents the greatness of this cleric. Allan Mandindi strongly believes that we all have greatness in us and is committed to using his achievements and experience to impact on other people's lives so they too can witness and become great and make massive contribution to the society.

As Mr Allan Mandindi has consistently engaged in positive action and he is actively transforming his community, we at Greatness University recognise him as worthy of the title *Creator of Greatness*.

Mrs Mireille Malu Mabika Mukumbay, DRC

Volunteer & Community Developer

Mrs Mireille Malu Mabika Mukumbay was born in 1973 in Kinshasa, Democratic Republic of Congo. She is married to Dr. Tshibangu Mukumbay, founder and leader of the political movement "Union du Peuple d'Avenir" (French) or "United People with One Destiny" (English). She graduated with a bachelors degree with honours in Psycho-Social studies from the University of East London which was inspired by her rich experience and knowledge in the field of social care. She worked as a bilingual officer with the local government. She is currently taking a Masters Degree in Children and Adolescent Mental Health.

Mrs Mukumbay's zeal for the welfare people is also reflected in her dedication for 20 years in volunteering to teach the youth at her local church, Sureway International Christian Ministries, where she is a highly esteemed member of staff who is often described as "loving, inspiring and passionate". Furthermore, her love for community and volunteering propelled her to serve as a Community Market Researcher for South Westminster Renewal Partnership by interviewing people from several backgrounds about their satisfaction with local services, the findings of which were essential and contributed in the improvement of the services provided by the organisation. Her achievements were all accomplished whilst being a full time mother of five and offering tremendous support to her husband in his political endeavours by travelling with him to various countries.

As she has consistently engaged in positive action and she is actively transforming her community, we at recognise Mrs Mireille Mukumbay as a *Creator of Greatness.*

Miss Antoinette Peters, UK

Freelance Fashion Designer

Antoinette is a freelance fashion designer who works part time on bespoke creative wear. Her past projects vary from bridal, occasion wear to casual contemporary trends, some of which has been in catwalk shows. She also works fulltime as a Project Officer with a local authority in the UK. Following on from her studies in fashion in Luton, London and Milan; Antoinette has worked as a designer specialising in hats, accessories, retail fashion management, account management, fashion management recruitment, and project management.

Antoinette was the crowned winner of Miss Creativity 2013 and award winner Miss Smile with New Level Pageants which lead to other international contests. She continues to use her gifts as a singer, songwriter, praise and worship leader, choir director. During her free time, she works as a volunteer for AZALEA which helps vulnerable women who are exploited. As an all-round creative, Antoinette draws, paints and designs bespoke greeting cards as an additional hobby.

As she has consistently engaged in positive action and she is actively transforming her community, we at Greatness University recognise Antoinette Peters as worthy of the title *Creator of Greatness.*

Dr Anana Phipher-Derilhomme, USA

Entrepreneur, Author, Speaker, Success Coach, and Mentor

www.blessedgirls.com

Anana is an Entrepreneur, Author, Speaker, Success Coach and Mentor to girls and women around the world. She is a Regional Statesmen of iChange Nations. Dr. Phifer-Derilhomme is the President & Founder of BlessedGirls: a Non-Profit Youth Leadership and Mentor Organization with a resourceful curriculum that educates girls and highlights female leaders from around the world to empower the youth to be the change agents needed in their community to end poverty and stand for equality. For more information visit www.blessedgirls.com

Recently named as International World Civility Ambassador for her wisdom and ability to direct important public issues regarding humanity and her work with girls and women globally, Dr Phifer-Derilhomme is the creator of the BlessedGirl Superhero - BGS (black teenage girl superhero). BGS is a cartoon character that educates, inspires and encourages girls to develop a positive self-image, business development, and community leadership.

Dr Phifer-Derilhomme is also the Founder, Coach and Trainer with Moms on A Mission. MOMS Organization trains woman to transform their lives with an online program "Mission I-AM Possible" where woman heal, grow, rejuvenate and stimulate their passion and fulfill their God-given purpose. She is privileged to work with a team of inspiring business partners in the United States, London, Canada, South America and USVI. She is a Certified John Maxwell Coach and Trainer with proven success strategies to help you design and develop the life you dream of. As a business and confidence coach, she helps people to get to thier BIG

WIN by being clear, confident and courageous about your purpose and destiny.

Dr Phifer-Derilhomme is a three-time author (A Mother's Love: Letters to Our Sons, Live Your Best Life: Answer the Call & BlessedGirl Superhero: Book of Affirmations). She is a dedicated wife and mother to 3 extraordinary young men. She is a sought for being an enthusiastic and accountable leader. As a professional speaker, mentored by Professor Dr. Ruben West-Black Belt Speakers Global & Ambassador Dr Clyde Rivers, she speaks at conferences, churches, and community events about the importance of personal development, entrepreneurship, community, and self-empowerment. Dr Phifer-Derilhomme has the gift and calling to get people see past their fears and limitations, overcome obstacles, and soar into Greatness.

As she has consistently engaged in positive action and she is actively transforming her community and the world, we at Greatness University recognise Dr Phifer-Derilhomme as worthy of the title Creator of Greatness.

Miss Alka Sharma, Canada

Founder of Alka's Total Fitness, Ballroom Dancer, and Author

www.alkastotalfitness.com

Alka Sharma is making waves in the fitness industry with her unique style and drive for a healthy lifestyle. Her three main passions in life are: dance, kickboxing and helping individuals reach their full potential by nurturing them to be passionate about health and fitness. Her own journey has been challenging as she struggled with weight, a lack of self-confidence and self-esteem in her formative years. That journey has inspired her to help other women aspire to a journey using insights she has gained on her own path. Her story is contained in her book *From Cocoon to CEO: Living the Life of Your Dreams.*

Alka is an accomplished Latin and ballroom dancer having competed both locally and internationally. She truly enjoyed the high of dance performance and training which led her journey into fitness world began. Alka's inspiration came from Gillian Michaels. Known for being on the show 'Biggest Loser', Gillian is dynamic, strong both physically and mentally. This is the character that Alka admires along with Gillian's tenacity and drive. This tenacity was apparent and very necessary when Alka launched her plan to create a studio for her fitness dream.

Alka's Total Fitness enables women to feel comfortable within smaller class size, programs that are customised for their needs and goals delivered by fully trained and caring instructors. For more information, visit www.alkastotalfitness.com

As Alka has consistently engaged in positive action and she is actively transforming her community, we recognise her as a Creator of Greatness.

Masters of Greatness

This award is given on merit to people who have researched greatness, documented it and published it with Greatness University Publishers.

Mr Karsten Wille, UK

International Speaker, Educator and Author

Karsten Wille holds a B.A (Hons) in History and Languages, and Post Graduate Degrees in Christian Ministry and Applied Theology. Karsten has worked as a Pentecostal Pastor planting churches in the UK and working in a Missions and Evangelism department ministering the Gospel in Africa, Asia and South America. With a PGCE from Exeter University and focused studies at the Open University in Educational Research, Karsten has taught Religious Education in schools for the past 20 years with a keen interest in apologetics.

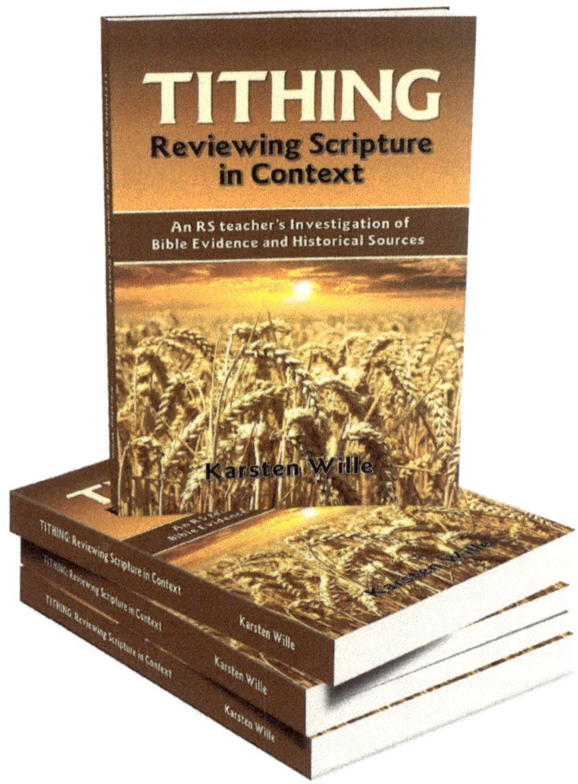

Karsten also speaks on Philosophy and Ethics at conferences and Bible Academies. He has contributed to Christian Radio for morning devotions and appeared on TV discussing the subject of Godly marriage. He is the author of Tithing: Reviewing Scripture in Context. As Karsten Wille has researched and published with Greatness University Publishers, we are honoured to recognise him as worthy of the title *Master of Greatness.*

Mrs Nadia Watson-Anthony, USA

Co-Founder of Christian Maturity, Greatness Researcher, Relationship Coach, and Author

Nadia Watson-Anthony graduated from Sunset Bible Institute with a Bachelor's degree in Biblical Studies. She also has a Bachelor of Science in Business Management from Amridge University. She is currently completing her Masters degree in Human Enrichment. She is the author of *H.E.R. Inspiration*: a 31-day devotional book. She is also the co-author of *Jesus Changed Our Lives, Les Brown Changed Our Lives, Women to Women*, and *The Book of Love*. Nadia is also the State Representative of Greatness University in Montana, USA.

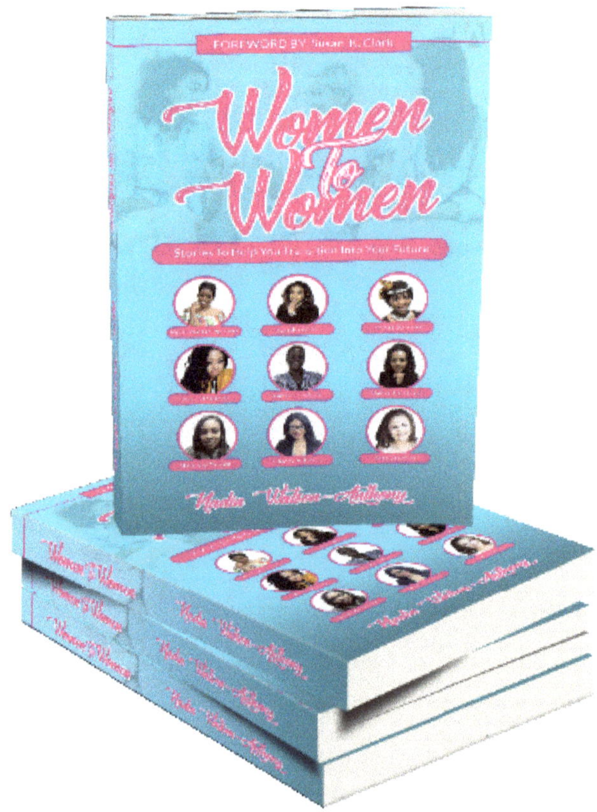

Nadia and her husband founded a mentorship program called "Christian Maturity" in which they apply their God giving gifts to put into practice their motto "We bring life to the living!"

As Nadia Watson-Anthony has researched and published with Greatness University Publishers, we are honoured to recognise her as worthy of the title *Master of Greatness*.

Mr Charles Anthony, USA

Evangelist, Marriage Counsellor, Author, and Co-Founder of Christian Maturity

Charles Anthony is a brilliant son, an incredible father and a devoted husband. He is an evangelist and a graduate of Sunset School of Preaching where he graduated with a Bachelor's degree in Biblical Studies. He is currently pursuing a Masters in Spiritual Leadership at the Sunset International Bible Institute. Charles is also a certified marriage counsellor.

Charles Anthony has co-authored three bestselling books: *Les Brown Changed Our Lives*, *Jesus Changed Our Lives*, and *The Book of Love*. Charles is also the State Representative of Greatness University in Montana, USA.

As Charles Anthony has researched and published with Greatness University Publishers, we are honoured to recognise him as worthy of the title *Master of Greatness*.

Mrs Tracy Norah Guma, UK

Co-Author of Yega Orutooro

Tracy Guma holds a Bachelor of Arts in Business Studies and Accounting from South Bank University, London. Since her graduation, Tracy has worked as a Civil Servant in various posts at key UK Government Departments.

She is the co-author of Yega Orulimi Orutooro: Learn Rutooro Language. Tracy's motivation and enthusiasm for co-authoring this book was driven by her love for Tooro as her birthplace, which offers a very rich language, heritage and culture not found anywhere else. Tracy herself is a fluent Rutooro speaker is encouraging fellow Batooro and all those interested in learning basic aspects of the language to utilize this publication as an opportunity to get started. As Tracy has researched and published with Greatness University Publishers, we are honoured to recognise her as worthy of the title *Master of Greatness.*

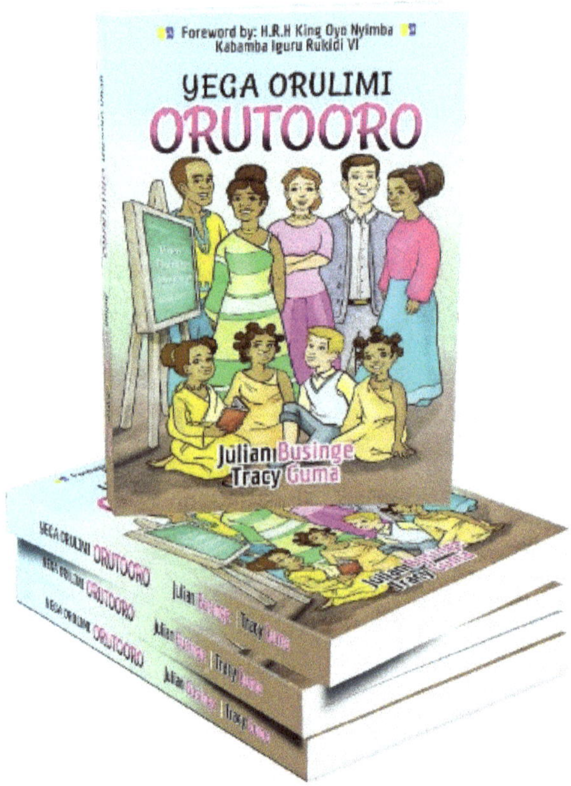

Mr Guma Komwiswa, UK

Co-Author of The Great Kingdom of Tooro

His Excellency Guma Komwiswa holds an MBA in Strategic Management. He has worked as a Senior Policy and Planning Consultant with the Ministry of Internal Affairs in Uganda. He is now the Chief of Protocol of Tooro Kingdom, Uganda. He also works as a Consular Officer at the Uganda High Commission in London, UK.

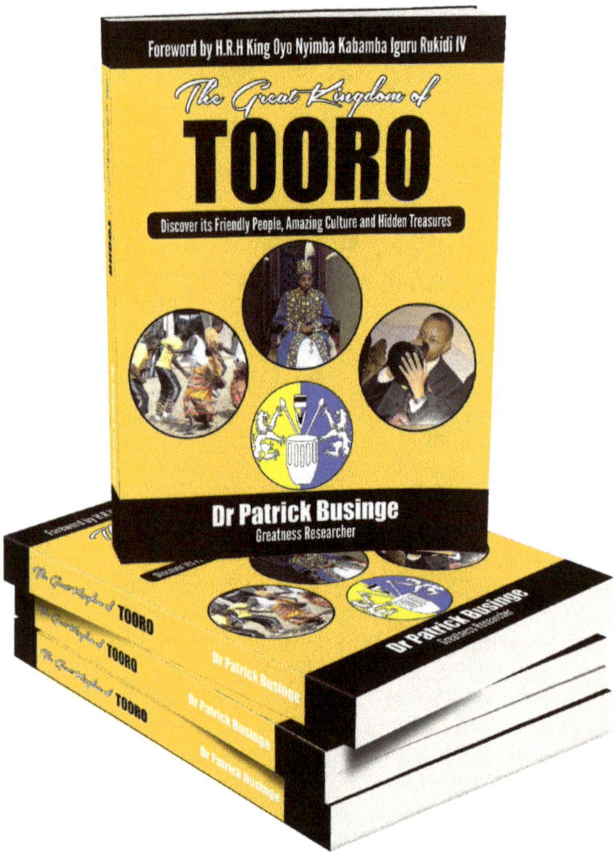

His Excellency Guma is also the co-author of *The Great Kingdom of Tooro*: a book that captures the friendly people, the amazing culture and the hidden treasures of Tooro Kingdom in Uganda that is currently ruled by the World's Youngest King.

As Guma Komwiswa has researched and published with Greatness University Publishers, we are honoured to recognise him as worthy of the title *Master of Greatness*.

Index by First Name

www.ingramcontent.com/pod-product-compliance
Lightning Source LLC
LaVergne TN
LVHW071334210926
848486LV00003B/146